"I enthusiastically recommend this grour
foundation in mentalization principle:
practice innovations which coherently
the MBT model. Clear descriptions of th
by vivid testimony from the young adults who used art therapy.
Much to value here for art therapists working with a range of client
groups."

—*Dr Neil Springham, consultant practice-research art therapist,
Oxleas NHS Trust, lead for psychological therapies and MBT services
(Bromley), previously Chair of British Association of Art Therapists*

"Mentalizing theory has finally found a therapeutic application
for client groups that it has not been able to reach in words alone.
This is the best practical guide for a clinical application that will, I
hope, generate practical support not just for our therapists but all
practitioners willing to step outside the frame of their traditional
boundaries. Everyone has much to learn from this excellent book."

—*Professor Peter Fonagy, OBE, FMedSci, FBA, FAcSS, PhD, DipPsy,
Head of the Division of Psychology and Language Sciences, UCL, and
Chief Executive, Anna Freud National Centre for Children & Families*

"This book is a gem. These talented clinicians and excellent
writers contribute substantially to their field by explicating a
richly psychotherapeutic approach to patients' expressive artwork.
The book is expertly curated with clinical examples and concrete
guidelines for structuring groups, all framed in a lucid articulation
of the mentalizing approach to treatment."

—*Jon G. Allen, PhD, Baylor College of
Medicine and The Menninger Clinic*

"Reading about theory-informed practice of mentalizing art therapy couldn't be any easier. *Mentalizing in Group Art Therapy* is a much-needed text that provides clear theory and practice of mentalizing in art therapy. The chapters build upon defining theory that leaves the reader with a sense of readiness to practice. Furthermore, the clearly illustrated examples of dialogue among clients, therapists, and artwork illuminate the practice of mentalizing in action. This book is a must for art therapists to self-reflect on their practice and hone their skills."

—*Megan Robb, ATR-BC, LPC, NCC, Director of the Art Therapy Counseling Graduate Program, Associate Professor in Art Therapy Counseling, Southern Illinois University, Edwardsville*

"Kula and Kate describe their exploration into the solid worth that mentalizing-based art therapy can bring. They provide art therapists and colleagues with a 'compass' to the MBAT. They describe several interventions and group discussions concerning how the process of making a tangible artwork can enhance mentalizing. A lovely hopeful book about youngsters in a 'tumultuous and critical stage of life.'"

—*Marianne Verfaille, art therapist, registered MBT-specialised therapist, and author of* Mentalizing in Arts Therapies

"Authors Moore and Marder have taken art therapy to a whole new level with the addition of the concept of Mentalizing. Here the authors demonstrate their work with patients through explication of mentalizing processes along with case examples of how to work with artistic metaphors to produce growth in self-understanding. This is a particularly valuable new volume in group mental health treatment."

—*Flynn O'Malley, PhD, ABPP, Senior Psychologist, The Menninger Clinic; Associate Professor, Dept. of Psychiatry and Behavioral Sciences, Baylor College of Medicine, Houston, Texas*

"Moore and Marder have authored a marvellous introduction to mentalizing in art therapy—not only well written, but easily understandable. This is no small feat because, while theoretically simple, mentalizing is also extremely complex. My thanks to Kula and Kate for an excellent adaptation of this approach for our profession."

—*Judith A. Rubin, PhD, ATR-BC, HLM,*
Editor, Approaches to Art Therapy

"Moore and Marder bring the power of art therapy, with a mentalizing approach, to emerging adult groups, in order to gain personal insight into self, and empathy towards others. This book is a must for anyone working with emerging adults. The interventions are innovative and easy to incorporate into your own personal practice. I plan to bring this information to my students so they can best serve this unique population."

—*Deborah Elkis-Abuhoff, PhD, LCAT, ATR-BC, ATCS,*
Associate Professor and Program Director,
Hofstra University Creative Arts Therapy Counseling

of related interest

Group Analytic Art Therapy
Gerry McNeill
ISBN 978 1 84310 301 1
eISBN 978 1 84642 457 1

DBT-Informed Art Therapy
Mindfulness, Cognitive Behavior Therapy, and the Creative Process
Susan M. Clark
ISBN 978 1 84905 733 2
eISBN 978 1 78450 103 7

Art Therapy and Substance Abuse
Enabling Recovery from Alcohol and Other Drug Addiction
Libby Schmanke
ISBN 978 1 84905 734 9
eISBN 978 1 78450 118 1

The Handbook of Art Therapy and Digital Technology
Edited by Cathy Malchiodi, PhD
Foreword by Dr. Val Huet
ISBN 978 1 78592 792 8
eISBN 978 1 78450 774 9

Mentalizing in Group Art Therapy

INTERVENTIONS FOR EMERGING ADULTS

Kula Moore and Kate Marder

Jessica Kingsley *Publishers*
London and Philadelphia

First published in 2020
by Jessica Kingsley Publishers
73 Collier Street
London N1 9BE, UK
and
400 Market Street, Suite 400
Philadelphia, PA 19106, USA

www.jkp.com

Library of Congress Cataloging in Publication Data
A CIP catalog record for this book is available from the Library of Congress

British Library Cataloguing in Publication Data
A CIP catalogue record for this book is available from the British Library

ISBN 978 1 78592 815 4
eISBN 978 1 78450 893 7

Printed and bound by CPI Group (UK) Ltd, Croydon, CR0 4YY

*To Augustus and Mamawa, my siblings, niecelings
and nephews. And to my Peter.*

Kula Moore

*To my husband Fadi and our loves, Fiona and Isaac.
To Shannon, Curt, and Emily, Al and Nahla, and to sweet Oscar.*

Kate Marder

Contents

List of Tables and Figures

Acknowledgments

We honor our patients for their humor, resilience, and courageous endeavors to explore and to understand and to accept and to change. These pages could not exist without them. We are extremely grateful for our colleagues at The Menninger Clinic, and for all the mentors and teachers who have encouraged us along the way. Menninger's emphasis on education and training offered remarkable exposure and opportunities to learn from the very best. For that we are grateful. We thank Jon Allen for his timely words of motivation and for welcoming two unknowing art therapists to sit in on his mentalizing groups. We appreciate Peter Fonagy's support for art therapy and his self-effacing guidance; and our friends across the pond at ICAPT (International Centre for Arts Psychotherapies Training), who opened up their work to us and brought us into the mentalizing fold. We thank our compassionate colleagues in the psychiatric rehabilitation department at Menninger for their unmatched ability to hold group spaces and wear all the hats. We thank the research department for graciously providing data. Warm thanks to Janice Poplack, for her gift of curating safe spaces and welcoming us in. We are grateful for Judy McGrath, who offered accountability and unrelenting confidence in our capacity to do this work. We have learned a lot from the many treatment teams we have been a part of over the years, and are especially grateful for teams Davidson, Kayatekin, and Ashraf, fervent champions for art therapy. Compass nurses, MHAs (mental health associates), social workers, psychologists, addictions and eating disorder specialists, we value your dedication to patients and their families. Finally, we thank

Flynn O'Malley and Patricia Daza for their unyielding support, in word and in deed, for the Compass mentalizing-based art therapy (MBAT) group and the production of this book.

Disclaimer

All art images, descriptions, and discussions are included with express written permission from patients. Dialogues in this book are not transcripts but reconstructions of the group discussion, based on vigorous note-taking and the recollection of the therapists. The narratives and group dialogues are not exact statements, but are true, in essence. We made every effort to maintain the integrity of those discussions, while protecting the confidentiality of our patients. All patient names used are pseudonyms and identifying information has been changed.

CHAPTER 1

Mentalizing

As art therapists, we noticed ourselves making numerous connections between art therapy and mentalizing, an approach advocated by our colleagues at The Menninger Clinic in Houston, Texas. Though this was a relatively new approach to us, the concept felt suspiciously obvious. As we learned more about mentalizing through discussions, meetings, trainings, and presentations, we realized that this was part of its charm. We were fortunate enough to have Peter Fonagy (who originated the theory of mentalization, co-developed mentalizing-based treatment (MBT) with Anthony Bateman, and is a consultant at The Menninger Clinic)[1] attend our supervision groups, where he described and role-played his approach to mentalizing in a natural and self-effacing way, consistent with its description as "the least novel therapeutic approach imaginable" (Allen and Fonagy 2006, p.24). This disarmed our suspicions and helped us to feel confident testing the mentalizing waters with our art therapy patients on the emerging adult unit, the Compass Program for Young Adults.[2] With more practice, we realized that mentalizing in action is often more challenging than how effortless Fonagy made it appear. Nevertheless, it was clear that applying a mentalizing framework to art therapy would benefit our patients and enhance our work with them.

---

1   See http://psychoanalysis.org.uk/our-authors-and-theorists/peter-fonagy
2   See www.menningerclinic.com/patients/compass-program-for-young-adults/
    what-to-expect

MBT has been described as both revolutionary and the *least novel* approach conceivable (Allen and Fonagy 2006). We appreciate this duality, finding merits in both aspects. Allen, Fonagy and Bateman (2008) propose "that mentalizing—attending to mental states in oneself and other—is *the most fundamental common factor* among all psychotherapeutic treatments" (p.1), and further emphasize that thoroughly understanding mentalizing is beneficial to all mental health providers. We believe that mentalizing is the common thread that weaves through all therapies, including art therapy. We are confident that other art therapists will find this approach useful and reinvigorating.

A note from Kula

I attended MBT training in Massachusetts in the winter of 2015. It was structured so that each section of the weekend-long training included informational lectures on a particular mentalizing topic, followed by demonstrations of the mentalizing stance by its founders, and culminating in opportunities for the clinician participants to practice mentalizing methods in a group role-play format. Despite my resolve to author this book, I am not naturally inclined to be the central focus of any group, large or small. At this training, that changed. Perhaps I was disoriented by the snow-covered northeast terrain (which was ravaged by a blizzard shortly before my arrival), or enchanted by the unfamiliar climate, or jolted by its stark contrast to the Houston humidity. Possibly due to an amalgamation of all of these, combined with my growing fascination with mentalizing, I was motivated to participate in the group role-play.

The founders and designated training hosts rotated from room to room as a group of about 12 participants practiced applying mentalizing concepts with volunteer students in the role of patients. I had a suspicion that they were under strict orders to embody the most difficult traits of borderline personality disorder (BPD) they had ever come into contact with, heard about, read about, or imagined. The role-play was organized as a tag team, so that when one clinician became stuck or came to a natural pause, another tagged in and took their place. One by one, the people I was in the room with—seasoned clinicians with decades more experience—became stuck. Under normal circumstances, I would have waited for everyone else to have a turn while praying to the God of all clocks, watches, and time-telling devices for the group to run out of time prior to my turn. I would have been prepared to wait it out; but, for aforementioned reasons, I was more open to displays of trial and inevitable error than my constitution typically permits. So I volunteered. As I both predicted and feared, I became stuck. I felt myself becoming flushed, although due to my Liberian genetics and consequent affinity for the sun, my face did not expose me. Moments before all words found hiding places in the corners of my mouth, refusing to move outward to form sound, a thought occurred to me: *I am an art therapist.* To my knowledge, I was the only art therapist at that particular conference, and certainly in that particular room. I looked into the havoc-wreaking, flickering eyes of the volunteer-student-patient and offered, "Why don't we make some art?" The room grew still. Then, I heard a British accent declare, "Well, that's not fair," followed by some laughter, my explanation that I am, indeed, an art therapist, and ultimately the next person taking the chair to continue to role-play.

This declaration of inequity, though made in jest, has rested with me. It sparked curiosity about professional otherness (I am familiar with otherness in various contexts), which I imagine many art therapists encounter. More directly, it widened my perspective of what art therapy has to offer to mentalizing, the rich potential of this work. More profoundly, it has added to my expanding gratitude for this tool that I have—that we art therapists have—to offer. It is a gift actually, for our patients and for us.

A note from Kate

After I accepted the psychiatric rehabilitation specialist position at The Menninger Clinic, I discussed the new job with a good friend, a social worker who studied with Dr. Fonagy at the Anna Freud National Centre for Children and Families. I do not remember her exact words but she mentioned that mentalizing is a treatment approach at Menninger. When I admitted that I was unfamiliar with the term *mentalizing*, she replied with something along the lines of, "Oh, it's kind of silly. It's basically just a fancy name for something all therapists do anyway." Despite learning more about it through discussions, presentations, and trainings at Menninger, this humorous introduction to mentalizing has stayed with me.

Although I still do not think my friend was completely wrong, I also wish I had known about mentalizing sooner. It was definitely not the approach taken by the treatment teams in the settings where I worked previously, including an adult inpatient psychiatric unit in New York City and a residential adolescent treatment program outside Washington, DC. As an art therapist who filled many roles, as art therapists often do, I provided recreation, leisure, wellness, and psychoeducational groups in addition to art therapy. I found that I sometimes had a different understanding of the patients than the doctors, psychologists, and social workers did. At times, I felt a lack of cohesion between the work being done in groups and the rest of treatment, and there was not always room for my observations in team discussions. Additionally, it often seemed like the patient's point of view was overlooked in case formulations. Perhaps what was missing was the common language and stance of curiosity, perspective taking, and open-mindedness that a mentalizing framework provides.

Over time, my career path has veered from the place and population where Kula and I developed the mentalizing-based art therapy (MBAT) group; yet, I find that mentalizing remains relevant regardless of the treatment setting, backgrounds, ages, and issues of the patients. MBT has provided a foundation from which my art therapy approach now stems. Whether in group or individual work, whatever I present to patients in art therapy now feels grounded in mentalizing, although this is not always explicitly discussed. Currently, I run a twice-weekly art therapy group in a different setting, a mixed-age adult outpatient program situated in a large hospital. I recently facilitated an art therapy group that took place following a Family Dynamics group where mentalizing was discussed.

As our group started, the patients asked what I thought of mentalizing, which prompted me to share about co-authoring this book. I mentioned that even if it is not the specific focus, mentalizing is a part of every group I lead, especially noticeable in the way we process the artwork. A more senior patient of the group commented, "I can see that." This led to a brief conversation about how we are mentalizing when we make the effort to take one another's perspective and to be curious when discussing the artwork. There were two new members present that day which can sometimes lead to less openness, but I did not find this to be the case. Instead, I felt patients making the effort to mentalize, asking questions, thinking about each other's mental states, and clarifying their own. Though this particular session did not involve one of the MBAT directives presented in this book, it served as a reminder that I proudly consider myself a mentalizing art therapist. Although I probably was mentalizing to some extent prior to learning about MBT, intentionally focusing on mentalizing has enhanced my practice. More importantly, I believe MBAT has positively impacted the experiences of patients I encounter.

An overview of mentalizing

When we explain mentalizing to the emerging adults of the Compass Program, it is simplified into *what*, *why*, and *how*. We explain to the patients that mentalizing is not only a part of the Compass group curriculum, but also the general treatment philosophy at Menninger, which is at its core a relational program. We tell them that they will hear about mentalizing in various parts of treatment: groups, individual therapy, family work, and in the treatment milieu. We say that our goal is no secret: the work of our program is increasing their capacity to mentalize, to offer opportunities to adopt a mentalizing stance in interactions with other people and in how they think about themselves. In order to do this, we need their help to engage actively and collaboratively in treatment. Patients are informed that mentalizing is an attitude, but it is also a skill that can be learned, practiced, and cultivated. Rarely do we go into depth about the neurobiological underpinnings of mentalizing, as we focus more on thoughts, feelings, and behaviors than the complex processes of the brain. At the same time, mentioning the growing neuroscience research often gives mentalizing more credence. Our patients also learn that mentalizing is a useful approach because it is the basis of secure attachments, and many emerging adults have difficulty navigating the inherent shifts in relationships during this life stage.

In these pages, it is our aim to identify the joints where mentalizing and art therapy meet, and to demonstrate the application of MBAT in an inpatient psychiatric group for emerging adults in the Compass Program. From a mentalizing framework, we focus on the therapeutic stance, therapist role, and key aims of treatment. We discuss the role of the art therapy process and product, addressing the facilitation of epistemic trust, salutogenesis, resilience, agency, and connection. Additionally, we provide a brief history of art therapy at The Menninger Clinic and a description of the current young adult treatment program, contextualizing the population and setting of our work.

What?

Simply stated, mentalizing is the idea of attending to states of mind in oneself and others, the practice of *holding mind in mind* (Allen *et al.* 2008). Mentalizing is typical of all people; it is generally within our human capacity to mentalize. When we try to make sense about what is going on in ourselves or in other people, we are mentalizing at a basic level. When we try to understand why a person has behaved in a certain way, when we interpret facial expressions and body language, when we give meaning to actions, we are mentalizing (Allen *et al.* 2008). This implicit mentalizing is natural and occurs without much thought. Implicit mentalizing is perceived, unconscious, nonverbal, and automatic. However, explicit mentalizing is interpreted, conscious, verbal, and reflective

(Allen *et al.* 2008; Fonagy, Bateman and Luyten 2012). We naturally mentalize implicitly, but we do not always mentalize well. Exclusive reliance on implicit mentalizing, such as failure to examine and clarify beliefs, can lead to interpersonal problems, reinforcing distorted or overly simplistic assumptions about self and others (Fonagy *et al.* 2012).

Anthony Bateman and Peter Fonagy developed MBT as an evidence-based treatment for people with BPD because deficits in mentalizing are characteristic of this disorder. MBT has since been applied to additional clinical issues, including mood disorders, eating disorders, addiction, and other personality disorders, as impaired mentalizing is a common thread in many psychiatric problems. MBT is not a specific school of psychotherapy, but a mechanism of change common across all therapies (Allen *et al.* 2008; Bateman and Fonagy 2016). Therapeutic programs commonly treat co-occurring disorders, and mentalizing-enhancing interventions are useful regardless of the specific brand or type of therapy adopted by administration to attract and treat patients (Allen *et al.* 2008). MBT aims to restore the balance between implicit and explicit mentalizing across various dimensions: cognitive and affective, internal and external, self and other (Bateman and Fonagy 2016; Fonagy *et al.* 2012). Practicing explicit mentalizing while in treatment offers opportunities for new, corrective, interpersonal experiences.

MBT is rooted in attachment theory, which was developed by Bowlby (1982) and Ainsworth (1989). The ability to mentalize is intimately linked with attachment style. When insecure attachments exist, caregivers are unable to reflect the child's state of mind; therefore the child does not receive caregiver modeling or feedback to develop the capacity to mentalize. When feedback to the child is either completely missing or inaccurate, the child is unable to fully develop the capacity to mentalize. The child does not learn how to understand thoughts, feelings, and motivations of self or others. The child lacks trust in the caregiver's reliability as a source of knowledge and does not view others as dependable resources for social information (Bateman and Fonagy 2016). Conversely, secure attachments can be conceptualized as those where mentalizing exists; and the capacity to mentalize develops through early parent–child interactions. Caregivers who can reflect on the child's intentions with accuracy help the child learn to regulate affect and develop a sense of his or her own mind (Fonagy *et al.* 2002). When caregivers demonstrate understanding of the child's experience and give feedback about that experience, they provide a useful mentalizing model. This helps the child learn how to pay attention to and understand what he or she is experiencing. The child learns to reflect upon and understand his or her own state of mind. This follows a progression from assisted to independent observation of self, which lays a foundation for emotion regulation and healthy engagement with others. Secure attachments allow us to trust others as reliable sources of knowledge. The process is dependent on healthy and consistent emotional interaction between the child and caregiver, and can only occur when mentalizing is present (Bateman and Fonagy 2016).

Given the strong link between mentalizing and attachment, it would stand to reason that the role of the mentalizing therapist is similar to the attachment functions of a primary caregiver (Allen 2013; Holmes 2006). Commonly accepted is the notion that the therapeutic alliance is the most important factor (Ardito and Rabellino 2011; Horvath and Symonds 1991; Lambert and Barley 2001), but there has been limited inquiry into the specific mechanisms of change in therapy. Bateman and his colleagues (2018) propose that effective therapies validate agency in patients and therefore stimulate mentalizing, enabling patients to use and benefit from techniques in therapy. Therapy works by changing the patient's attitude toward social learning. Mentalizing on the therapist's part helps the patient feel felt, and not only builds therapeutic alliance, but also shifts receptiveness to new information outside of therapy (Bateman and Fonagy 2012a; Bateman *et al.* 2018). Art therapy has the potential to enhance this process, opening new pathways to communication and social learning.

The following example emphasizes the significance of attachment relationships. For many emerging adults, the magnitude of attachment is extensive, impacting functioning during this stage of life and beyond. In art therapy, Christie explored her attachment relationship with her mother. When mentioned in conversation, she spoke about feeling sorry for her mother but also angry with her for not having a voice in the family. Christie's father worked out of the home and was not physically present most of the time. Christie's mother, who was present, struggled with mental health issues. From Christie's perspective, her mother allowed herself to be infantilized, essentially giving up her voice so that Christie's father could make all the decisions. Because she was currently hospitalized, Christie feared that her father and brothers would view her as they did her mother: incapable of making sound decisions.

Christie recalled being a young child and feeling an intense longing for her mother, even when she was nearby in the next room. She noted that she did not go to her mother during these times, and wondered if she could sense then that her mother was not emotionally available to her or able to soothe or meet her needs. Christie was invited to create an image of a relationship and chose her mother (see Figure 1.1). She drew herself as a child sitting with a hand emanating from the center of her chest, reaching toward her mother but not quite touching her. The hand becomes limp just as it gets close to the mother. The figure Christie drew to represent her mother initially had no mouth. Christie decided later to add a small, closed mouth, noting that her mother did have a voice but seemed anxious when using it because of being silenced by her father for so long. In the image, Christie's mother's arms are folded and she is not facing Christie, nor is Christie looking toward her mother, although her body is slightly angled in her mother's direction. She explained that though she longed for her mother, she often acted like she did not need her. There are eyes in the drawing representing other family members, who she described as critical and judgmental of both Christie and her mother.

In Christie's case, her insecure attachment style seemed to have developed in part from her early family environment. She experienced her primary caregivers as emotionally unreliable and physically unavailable. This attachment style created challenges with feeling safe and trusting others in relationships. In fact, she experienced close relationships as threatening, with the potential for abandonment, rejection, criticism, and attempts to control her. As a result, Christie hid herself from others, including family members and friends, and sought comfort in substances to manage her feelings. She preemptively rejected others before they could reject her for her perceived weaknesses, which she made great efforts to hide. This disconnection from others and from her own emotions was reinforced by her deep-rooted fear of becoming like her mother, the identified sick person in the family. Christie's feelings of shame and inadequacy made it difficult for her to share her thoughts and emotions, further isolating her from meaningful connections.

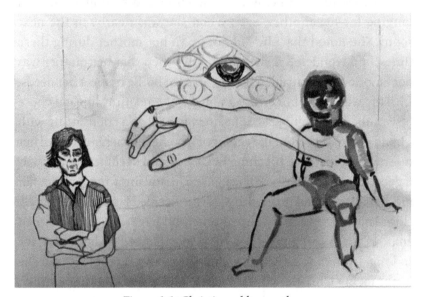

Figure 1.1. Christie and her mother

Why?

If improving mentalizing capacity is an identified goal of treatment, it rests on the premise that this faculty is somehow diminished for people in treatment. For many of our patients, this assumption holds true. More broadly, for all humans mentalizing capacity fluctuates and is thus compromised at times. In distress, it may be difficult to stop and think. Many of the young people in the Compass Program arrive in a heightened or lowered state of emotional arousal, highly anxious and dysregulated, or severely depressed and avoidant. Mentalizing deficits are a hallmark in many psychiatric disorders, specifically personality disorders, which innately propagate distorted thinking, mental inflexibility, and lack of attentiveness to the minds and experiences of others (Allen 2003; Bateman and Fonagy 2012b, 2016; Bateman *et al.* 2018). Moreover, mentalizing deficits perpetuate relationship issues and can leave many young adults feeling disconnected and fearful about how to manage shifting relationship dynamics in this tenuous developmental period.

When we make the case for mentalizing to emerging adult patients, we let them know that mentalizing is about understanding self and others. It fosters healthy relationships and moves us away from making hasty assumptions, fixed and rigid ways of thinking, impulsivity, and reactivity. Mentalizing is the Compass approach because it helps emerging adults learn to take responsibility for their choices and actions, and ultimately develop a perception of self that is cohesive and agentive. From a mentalizing stance, it is unhelpful to assume that the intention or meaning behind a certain behavior is known without further exploration of other potential motivators and causes. Our aim is to encourage the practice of examining perceptions about what drives the actions of others, as well as how we interpret our own actions. Furthermore, it is vital to learn about, discuss, and practice mentalizing explicitly in treatment because it is most difficult to do when it is most needed—that is, in times of distress (Allen *et al.* 2008). One of our goals on Compass is to facilitate positive experiences of mentalizing, of understanding others and being understood while feeling the mentalizing efforts of others. We hope that patients can draw from these experiences in times of need.

How?

Therapists help patients learn about how they think and feel about themselves and others, how that shapes their responses to others, and how errors in understanding self and others may lead to inappropriate actions. The mentalizing therapist is not focused on changing behavior, working to provide insight, or engaging in cognitive restructuring. Mental processes remain the focus of this approach; however, changes occur consequently, as favorable side effects of mentalizing. These positive changes, encouraged by mentalizing interventions, facilitate further change in thoughts, feelings, and behaviors. Good outcomes are also indicated by improvements in the patient's ability to mentalize (Allen *et al.* 2008; Bateman and Fonagy 2012a).

While mentalizing is not a technique-based or acronym-infused therapy, there are teachable skills that help to incite mentalizing, which patients are encouraged to use in various areas of treatment:

- *Transparency:* Explicitly make thoughts and feelings known to others, allowing for open understanding. The rationale for transparency is that the mind is opaque, and so it is not useful to assume that others can know our exact thoughts and feelings or anticipate needs appropriately without some transparency. In the same way, it is difficult to assume thoughts and feelings and intentions of others without some transparency on their part.

- *Attitude of not knowing:* Maintain a flexible, open mindset with respect for the opacity of the mind: "You are not the expert on anyone else's mind."

- *Curious stance:* Question initial thoughts and feelings to consider what may be beneath the surface. Imagine a detective or scientist looking around, under, above, inside a thing before coming to a conclusion about what the thing is. Language like, "I wonder…" "I'm curious about…" "Help me understand…" is encouraged.

- *Pause button:* Stop the action in times of intense emotions to allow for time to pause and think.

- *Sit with feelings:* Identify, acknowledge, and accept difficult emotions without acting on them.

- *Clarify assumptions:* Check perceptions by asking clarifying questions.

- *Identify 90/10 situations:* Encourage reflection on how the past impacts the present. The 90/10 rule postulates that 90 percent of our response is based on past experience while 10 percent is about what is happening in the here and now. The numbers are arbitrary but skewed in order to call attention to the likelihood of distortion in stressful situations.

- *Identify nonmentalizing language:* Listen for red flag words like *always, only, never, just, everyone, nobody*, etc. These connote absolute certainty, and if already certain, there is no space for curiosity. Without curiosity, mentalizing is halted.

These skills are described as conduits for mentalizing, and many are detailed in the various mentalizing manuals and handbooks written for clinicians (Allen *et al.* 2008; Bateman and Fonagy 2012a, 2016). When we provide this condensed list of skills on Compass, we encourage patients to practice using them in interactions with peers, treatment providers, and family members. A recurring concern is whether we are teaching patients to engage in explicit mentalizing or teaching them to regurgitate the definition and terms associated with mentalizing. These doubts are quieted when patients hold mirrors back up to us, noticing our lapses in mentalizing. Once in a while, a patient will raise an open palm and mimic, "hit the pause button," or inform, "you said 'never' and that is nonmentalizing." These moments are usually followed by laughter, admissions of guilt, and a prevailing sense of unity in our humanity.

CHAPTER 2

Mentalizing-based Art Therapy

Background, Aims, and Application

We are imbued with appreciation for our art therapy colleagues in the United Kingdom for the knowledge and support received in the early stages of this work. During one of Peter Fonagy's visits to The Menninger Clinic, we were introduced to the work of expressive arts therapists at the International Centre for Arts Psychotherapies Training (ICAPT). This connection cultivated our curiosity about mentalizing and provided a sound base from which we could model and develop our program. Though many systemic differences exist—in healthcare generally and the treatment structure specifically—between our program and that of the arts psychotherapists abroad, we found mentalizing to be unifying. The mentalization approach provided a straightforward framework for use with a similar population, people with personality disorders. We were inspired by their enduring enthusiasm for an approach that was not as new and shiny to them as it was to us. It motivated us to push forward through the challenges inherent in this work.

Predecessors

The expressive arts therapists at ICAPT, and several others, have emphasized the ways in which art therapy is uniquely positioned to promote the depth and richness of mentalizing. The use of visual imagery in addition to verbal processing can enhance mentalizing due to the production of tangible artifacts to represent internal states (Springham *et al.* 2012; Taylor-Buck and Havsteen-Franklin 2013; Verfaille 2016). We have also found this to be true in our art therapy groups with emerging adults. Havsteen-Franklin (2016, p.145) describes how in MBAT, a patient engages in art making alongside another who is "contingently responsive, attuned, and curious so that the image can be understood in terms of what is happening in the person's immediate relationships, in the therapy and in current interpersonal contexts." In her work with children, Shore (2013) emphasizes the mentalizing processes involved in addressing attachment issues. Through art, children can symbolize overwhelming traumatic experiences and work through them to create coherent narratives, and ultimately make sense of confusing emotions.

Several art therapists have applied mentalizing to their work, primarily with adult outpatient populations. Taylor-Buck and Havsteen-Franklin (2013) discuss how the art-making process aids in the development of epistemic trust. They view the artwork as a source of communication and a contingent symbol of the creator's internal world. They also discuss the processes of joint engagement, noting that mentalizing may be increased when therapist and patient create alongside one another, engaging in a shared task. Joint engagement also encompasses the collective focus on the physical art object, looking with another (or others in group settings) at an externalized self object. Similarly, Springham *et al.* (2012) also emphasize the importance of the artwork as an externalized form of mental content, and as a focus of attention allowing patients to slow down to reflect and engage explicit mentalizing.

Greenwood (2012) illustrates how outpatient art therapy groups address negative symptoms of schizophrenia. She points to the capability of art to restore mentalizing processes, and credits increased understanding of her work to a mentalization framework. Similarly, Michaelides (2014) examines negative reflective functioning in a patient diagnosed with schizophrenia. She tests

Karterud and Pederson's (2004) hypothesis that art therapy is a way to safely explore the mind. Michaelides finds that the group's process of discussing the patient's artwork and imagining mental states contributing to the creation of the image helped the patient to develop mentalizing within himself. He was visible in the minds of the group members, and came to recognize that through their interest in his artwork. Franks and Whittaker (2007) present a pilot study about the effects of mentalizing in group art therapy for adults with personality disorders. Their findings indicate benefits for those in group art psychotherapy combined with individual verbal psychotherapy. Art therapy allows patients to explore visual perceptions safely before verbal acceptance and ownership. Franks and Whittaker (2007) emphasize that the art serves as a way for patients to make themselves known, demystifying interpersonal interactions that can be unpredictable for many people with personality disorders.

The goal of MBAT is to promote mentalizing about self, others, and relationships. Mentalizing involves reflection and interpretation of mental states and their impact on behavior (Allen *et al.* 2008). As demonstrated by our predecessors, art therapy invites individuals to depict their inner experience—feelings, perceptions, and imagination—through art making, which serves as a catalyst for mentalizing.

The role of the image: Mentalizing together

One way art therapy facilitates these mentalizing aims is through the creation of artwork in sessions. Art therapy naturally encourages mentalizing, because the patient reveals self through the image and relates to the images of others, using imagination to reflect on mental states. During an art therapy group, the patient's internal world is externalized by art making in addition to the therapeutic relationship and relationships with other group members (Malchiodi 2007; Wadeson 2010). Art therapy is commonly delivered in group formats, which provide an abundance of material. However, group art therapy is difficult to describe due to the multiple layers of contact between art therapist(s), patients, and artworks. Mentalizing as a framework organizes both patients and therapists around a common focus in the presence of complex interactions.

The art product is used to gain clarity around mental states, as it provides an opportunity to explore thoughts and feelings, and allows for consideration of multiple perspectives (Greenwood 2012; Havsteen-Franklin 2016; Taylor-Buck and Havsteen-Franklin 2013; Verfaille 2016). Helping patients develop and maintain curiosity and flexibility about their thoughts and emotions and those of others, while remaining "within grounded perspectives of self and others" (Havsteen-Franklin 2016, p.145), is an important component of MBAT. The artwork is used to help focus group members, who are encouraged to attend, to be curious about, and respond to each image. In this way the group members explore the image to help each patient mentalize their own thoughts, beliefs, emotions, and desires (Havsteen-Franklin 2016).

The image is a vehicle for mentalizing and serves to link one group member to another. It is the target of shared attention and slows the group down for structured reflection (Springham and Camic 2017). It is removed from the patient who created it, an externalized object, providing distance and safety. The artwork develops as a *second order representation*, an interpretation of reality with an *as if* quality that is not reality itself. Art making allows for imagination, experimentation, and the ability to play with mental representations safely, without the fear of impacting actual reality. The artwork provides the opportunity for patients to imagine alternatives and consider possibilities before taking action (Springham and Huet 2018; Springham *et al.* 2012; Verfaille 2016). When people are able to envision mental states in self and others, they become increasingly able to engage in secure relationships, connecting to others while simultaneously maintaining a separate, autonomous mind (Fonagy *et al.* 2012).

Metaphors are an important aspect of both mentalizing interventions and art therapy interventions. They have become a natural focus in the Compass MBAT group. The act of creating a metaphor requires mentalizing, as patients are asked to think about their own minds (Allen *et al*. 2012). Interpreting metaphors also involves mentalizing, as it requires imagination, exploration, and mental flexibility (Allen *et al*. 2008). Metaphors create safety as indirect expressions with multiple interpretations, less confrontational or threatening than making direct statements. Some patients in the MBAT group stay in the art metaphor when discussing their image. When direct questions are asked about a patient's experience, the patient has the freedom to confirm, deny, or clarify another's perceptions of the artwork. For example, a group member might say, "I would feel sad if I was in that image." The patient might agree with feelings of sadness, or clarify by stating, "I can see that, but for me it is more a feeling of confusion and frustration than sadness." The artwork provides access to layers of meaning that the group can help the patient uncover. Patients share their narrative through art making and begin making sense of it.

The mentalizing art therapist

The mentalizing art therapist is a supportive guide, attending, reflecting, and clarifying in order to help patients engage in mentalizing about their thoughts, desires, beliefs, emotions, and experiences. Mentalizing art therapists demonstrate a nonjudgmental, open-minded, and curious approach to mental states. Bateman and Fonagy (2010, p.13) further detail the mentalizing stance, including the following therapeutic components:

> a) humility deriving from a sense of "not-knowing"; b) patience in taking time to identify differences in perspectives; c) legitimizing and accepting different perspectives; d) actively questioning the patient about his/her experience—asking for detailed descriptions of experience ("what questions") rather than explanations ("why questions"); e) careful eschewing of the need to understand what makes no sense (i.e., saying explicitly that something is unclear).

Mentalizing art therapists demonstrate a flexible, open mindset with respect for the opacity of the mind and attentiveness to mental states. They do not have hierarchical rank over the group members, and therefore offer a perspective as another set of eyes looking *with* the other patients at the artwork (Springham *et al.* 2012). Mentalizing art therapists acknowledge that they are not the expert on the patient's mind or their artwork. As such, they must model an attitude of *not knowing* (Bateman and Fonagy 2010; Havsteen-Franklin 2016). Additionally, mentalizing art therapists express genuine interest in the patient's internal world, and demonstrate inquisitiveness by asking questions. These include questions about the patient's experience of making art, about their image and artistic choices, about their current thoughts and feelings and those expressed in the artwork, and about their experience of sharing their artwork and participating in the group. Mentalizing art therapists work to explore and clarify assumptions, encouraging consideration of what lurks beneath the surface.

Mentalizing art therapists adopt an active stance and work to generate and maintain mentalizing in the group. They share their impressions as a way of offering different ideas and encouraging group members to consider alternative perspectives about the motives of others (Karterud and Bateman 2012).

Karterud and Bateman (2012) identified key questions to consider when evaluating an MBAT group, which are assessed at group level and in terms of therapist interventions:

- Are most of the group members engaged in mentalizing in the here and now?

- Is nonmentalizing challenged?

- Is there a focus on affect as it links to current interpersonal interactions?

- Does curiosity and the discovery process supersede obtaining insight and offering advice?

Mentalizing art therapists' nonverbal indications and explicit articulation of interest in the artwork is particularly useful for patients with personality disorders, who may struggle with *mindblindness* or lack of attentiveness to the minds of others or their own (Allen *et al.* 2008; Baron-Cohen 1995; Bateman and Fonagy 2016; Springham and Camic 2017). For these patients, passivity on the part of the therapist can be damaging to the mentalizing group process. In a study examining group art therapy in MBT programs in the United Kingdom, Springham and Camic (2017, p.13) found that "the more demonstrative the art therapist was in indicating their genuine interest toward the artwork as a concrete object, including physically looking at it with explicit references to how their mind was viewing it, the more settled the group became in joining that focus of attention." Mentalizing art therapists initially focus the group on the artwork and ask reflective questions, but as the group grows in maturity and cohesion, patients come to share responsibility for those tasks. Even when patients increase autonomy in the art therapy group process, mentalizing art therapists remain active, engaging focus on the artwork as the shared target of attention (Springham and Camic 2017; Springham *et al.* 2012).

Mentalizing art therapists also facilitate mentalizing through transparency, modeling mentalizing for patients by sharing their own minds—thoughts, emotions, and curiosities—and marking these as their own. This process may be enhanced through the making and sharing of artwork by the art therapist (Springham *et al.* 2012; Taylor-Buck and Havsteen-Franklin 2013). When art therapists create artwork in the session, it also helps to level the playing field. For example, within the structure of a psychiatric hospital, the art therapist role is multifaceted and includes making decisions with the treatment team, so avoiding the pre-existing hierarchy in hospital settings is not always possible. When art therapists make art within the art therapy group, it creates a sense of togetherness and suspends the hierarchy for that time period. We find that Compass patients often express appreciation that art therapists engage in art making alongside them, even when time limitations of the group do not allow for exploration of the therapists' images. It is critical to emphasize the gravity and necessity of maintaining professional boundaries, even while demonstrating transparency. When therapists are able to share about their own artwork appropriately and invite patients to mentalize with them, it creates a deeper sense of cohesion and can lead to greater transparency from the patients.

Ultimately, the work of mentalizing art therapists is to generate mentalizing. They help patients differentiate self and others; move from implicit, automatic mentalizing to explicit, controlled mentalizing; challenge automatic assumptions; and elaborate internal representations of mental states. They demonstrate curiosity and help patients explore thoughts and emotions underpinning behaviors (Bateman and Fonagy 2016). Therapists must strive to see the world from the patient's vantage and authentically validate their experience. The therapist's role is to understand, and this cannot happen until mentalizing is activated. Additionally, therapists must monitor their own mentalizing, and recognize that this capacity is constantly at risk in the presence of nonmentalizing patients. It is important to take responsibility for mentalizing failures and lapses (Bateman and Fonagy 2012a), which we address later in this chapter.

Building epistemic trust

At an early age, we learn to receive information transferred by social communication from primary caregivers. This capacity is facilitated by epistemic trust, the ability to accept cultural knowledge transferred via social contact (Bateman and Fonagy 2016; Fonagy, Luyten and Allison 2015; Fonagy et al. 2017). Attachment is interwoven with this capacity, as our epistemic states are highly influenced by attachment history. Attachment relationships open us up to accepting information as credible and relevant. Ostensive cues (like eye contact, tone of voice, or contingent responsiveness) prepare us to receive information and minimize epistemic vigilance so we believe the information is relevant to us, generalizable to other situations, and worthy of remembering. From infancy, humans are wired to respond to ostensive cues (Csibra and Gergely 2011), which aids in the development of epistemic trust and recognizes the recipient as an agentive being with individual motives and intentions (Bateman and Fonagy 2016; Fonagy et al. 2015). From secure attachment bases, we come to rely on the authority of the person communicating and believe them. We can internalize the information, retain it, and apply it to other contexts. This process helps us to learn about the world and ourselves. It enables mentalizing and makes us better equipped to recognize others, learn from them, and appropriately navigate the social world.

Many Compass patients face challenges discerning epistemic trustworthiness. Early attachment relationship failures impede openness to social communication. The question, *can this person be trusted?*, is fraught with confusion and anxiety. Though epistemic vigilance is adaptive and can help to protect us from harmful situations, it can lead to epistemic mistrust, closing off the mind from receiving new information (Bateman *et al.* 2018). Epistemic mistrust impedes the process of updating knowledge about the social world. There is, in effect, a hunger for knowledge coupled with inability to trust what is received. People with chronic mistrust are not able to mentalize. They tend to avoid mental states, misrepresent how others perceive them, or have an inaccurate view of themselves. Inappropriate trust presents another problem. Patients who are overly trusting and have diffuse boundaries between self and others often take in all perceptions offered without question and develop a pattern of unhealthy relationships (Bateman *et al.* 2018; Bateman and Fonagy 2016; Fonagy *et al.* 2017). This diminished capacity to benefit from the social world can be extremely isolating for emerging adults.

Epistemic mistrust is illustrated by the case of Timothy, who was admitted to Compass after withdrawing from his second year of college. In addition to a preliminary post-traumatic stress disorder (PTSD) diagnosis upon admission due to sexual assault at the hands of a mentor followed by assault in a romantic relationship, Timothy also had a history of early attachment trauma. His parents both seemed misattuned to Timothy's emotions and experiences. Timothy's mother presented as anxious and disconnected, wanting for treatment to provide a "fix" to Timothy's challenges, and demonstrating an inability to tolerate his distress. This manifested as frequent phone calls to the nursing staff or treatment team, urging them to action at the slightest sign of discomfort experienced by Timothy; the mother's anxiety often surpassed Timothy's. However, the team recognized Timothy's contribution to the dynamic. He admitted to frequent phone calls with his mother to air grievances, while simultaneously denying problems when asked by the treatment team. Timothy's father was misattuned in a different way. He was experienced by the social worker in family calls as "all business," dismissive of Timothy and on occasion, devaluing of the social worker. Family work tended to focus on containing the mother's anxiety and father's impatience, and educating both parents on how to validate Timothy and give him space to have his own thoughts, emotions, and mind about his experiences.

Both parents struggled to meet Timothy's attachment needs, and it seemed difficult for him to communicate his needs to staff. Timothy often vacillated between dysregulation in situations when his emotions seemed excessive and out of control, or he shut down, reporting numbness and disconnection. His frequent somatic complaints, panic attacks, and "zoning out" in response to unknown triggers and stimuli seemed puzzling to staff, but provided a general acknowledgment of his need for nurturing and attunement.

Timothy was referred to the art therapy group and engaged in the process throughout hospitalization. As he describes his drawing of his relationship with self, Timothy strikingly captures difficulties with epistemic trust (Figure 2.1).

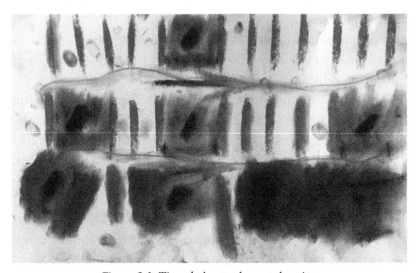

Figure 2.1. Timothy's attachment drawing

The following is a reconstruction of the group dialogue about Timothy's artwork.

Therapist: What have you got there, Timothy?

Timothy: What I was trying to make here is a timeline. For me, each of these little round parts of the drawing represents trauma. There is a soft blue-green color surrounding the visceral red inside each circle. There's comfort in the lighter blues and the greens, because all my traumas come from people that I trust. It's like they had this layer around them telling me, "it will be fine, we can be trusted," but then you get to the middle [and] it's red.

Group member #1: I notice there are several lines. What do they represent?

Timothy: Train of thought and time.

Therapist: You described the small red circular shapes as visceral. What does the red feel like?

Timothy: Painful. Like wow, people can really hurt you. And as the timeline continues, there are more circles, but the reality is, it's not that the same traumas are coming up more and more and more, there's not multiple exponentially increasing instances of trauma; it's just that one instance corrupts your current thoughts toward yourself.

Therapist: How do you mean?

Timothy: I talked about this in individual therapy today. Part of the reason I'm so hard on myself and don't believe that others will actually like me or be friends with me is that I'm trying to protect myself from potentially more trauma, since it came from these round, soft things [*pointing to drawing*]— the people who I trusted.

Group member #2: The sense of being haunted really comes through here. For me, when I look at it there's this eerie feeling.

And when you described the visceral red center, I connected with that. [*Wincing*] To me, it looks like it feels painful, like a wound.

Timothy: Yeah, extremely painful! It's also meant to be like an eyeball because it feels like my previous abusers are always watching me and still have this outer soft shell that made me think I could trust them. Even now sometimes I think, okay, maybe it would be okay to talk to those people again. But it still has the visceral red in the middle because I know what it could do.

Therapist: And what's that like for you, Timothy, when you think you could trust them?

Timothy: Scary. Like, how could I think that? I know how bad they hurt me. I was there! So that part just confuses the hell out of me.

Group member #1: That confuses me, too. It's like you know a fire will burn you but you keep going back to it, looking for warmth or something. But then you get burned. I do that all the time.

Timothy: Yeah, it really just messes with how I trust myself or connect with other people.

Therapist: In what way?

Timothy: It makes it extremely hard. Every aspect of thinking about myself, thinking about other people, the relationships with them, all of that is cloudy and foggy behind these experiences. I find I'm very slow to trust people, even my girlfriend. We've been dating for a year now and I still am convinced that she is only with me for an ulterior motive to get something out of me. I'm waiting for the day when she starts being abusive and terrible to me. I still have that fear with even my closest friends, too. It's like I can never fully trust people. And that's exhausting to be constantly worried about that.

Group member #2: Yeah, I'm usually on the lookout too. I'm just waiting for people to hurt me and not really fully able to relax.

Timothy: If you ever watch me in the group therapies, I'm constantly looking around the room and behind myself because I'm very vigilant.

Therapist: Really? I was wondering how that shows up here, in treatment, if it does.

Timothy: Yeah, it does. Even though I've forced myself in therapy to try to trust and talk to my team because they're professionals and here to help. And even then it's taken me a while to come to these conclusions about my emotions and how I perceive them, and why I perceive them, why I have these negative self-thoughts. It's taken me a while to trust my therapist enough to talk about why I think like I do.

Therapist: I think it is understandable that it would take a while to trust, considering that you have had these serious traumas [*pointing to drawing*].

Group member #3: I get the sense that you're trying to move past everything. The lines keep going, even after the traumas, up to that last part of the drawing.

Timothy: It feels like moving through molasses. But the last part of it is foggy and all mixed up. That's what my mind feels like now.

Group member #1: Can you help me understand, how this [*pointing to drawing*] relates to your relationship with yourself? I mean, how does this connect to what you said about having a negative view of yourself?

Timothy: If I'm hard on myself and very self-critical and putting myself down, I give myself a reason to distance from other people because I'm not worth their time. By thinking that, I'm preemptively protecting myself. I'm making myself feel bad so I'll push myself away from people because I can't get close.

Group member #3: And if you can't get close, then you can't get hurt?

Timothy: Right.

Group member #1: So it's like, if I'm unworthy, then I don't have to get close to people. And if I'm not close to people, then they can't hurt me.

Timothy: Right. And I'm still coming to terms with my past trauma. I'm still trying to understand it, but I think that's probably why I think that way. Right now, since I'm just uncovering all this stuff and figuring out myself, this is what I feel like right now, like a foggy explosion [*pointing to the bottom right corner of the drawing*]. But that's not where I will be forever. Maybe. Hopefully.

Therapist: What's it like for you when you're sharing this with the group and getting feedback?

Timothy: It's hard. I'm not used to talking about this, but this is easier because I'm talking about what I drew.

As Timothy's experience attests, the ability to trust is undermined by trauma. Timothy's image spurred a discussion about his difficulty trusting the treatment team, his girlfriend, and even himself. He identified emotions and acknowledged that the artwork provided safety, allowing him to speak about the impact of his trauma. Group members offered curiosity and validation for Timothy's experiences.

Mentalizing generates epistemic trust, and epistemic trust creates conditions for mentalizing. When a person responds to us sensitively, understands our personal narrative and we perceive that understanding, there is an epistemic match (Bateman and Fonagy 2016). Our work on Compass involves helping emerging adults to gradually regain and establish epistemic trust to draw them out from isolation. When we recognize the person's narrative, we help them recreate trust in the social world. By being mentalized, patients can learn to better mentalize themselves and others.

Art therapy supports the generation of health by fostering epistemic trust and ostensive communication (Springham and Huet 2018; Taylor-Buck and Havsteen-Franklin 2013). The production of art objects provides an opportunity for patients to make themselves known to others safely. The art therapy process helps to establish a developmental narrative of problems and offers a means for self-examination from the outside in. The artwork connects group members by providing a way to see each person's experience and attune to emotions presented. The curious stance encouraged in the group helps patients regain the capacity to be interested in the mental states of others and ultimately learn from others, reopening epistemic pathways. This may facilitate more appreciation of self and others and initiate the re-emergence of trust in the social world. By visually sharing experiences, patients feel recognized, understood, and empowered to make choices that can facilitate change in the course of their life paths.

Art is a valuable mode of transferring culturally relevant information between people, and thus a form of ostensive communication. Art is an encounter that can enhance mentalizing because it involves attachment. External art objects "offer a congruent medium for minds to encounter each other through mirroring" (Springham and Huet 2018, p.7). Through the art therapy process, patients can acquire the capacity to respond to these ostensive cues, and thus reconnect with the social environment. Epistemic trust lays the foundation for fostering salutogenesis, developing resilience, promoting agency and social connection, and encouraging empathy.

Fostering salutogenesis

During the first Art of Mentalizing Conference in New York, expressive therapies were described as *salutogenic*, natural supporters of health and wellbeing. Similar to art therapy, salutogenesis is an assets approach that focuses on what makes people healthy and promotes reconnecting to the social environment. It provides a valuable way of understanding and improving a person's adaptive capacity (Antonovsky 1979). Salutogenesis proposes that the way people view life impacts their *sense of coherence*, or how they are oriented to the world. Sense of coherence is a way of thinking and acting with internal trust, which allows people to identify and make use of environmental resources (Antonovsky 1996; Eriksson and Lindstrom 2005). Antonovsky proposed that when confronted with a stressor, a person with a strong sense of coherence will comprehend the challenge, believe that resources are available to help cope, and have desire and motivation to cope. Thus, sense of coherence is understood in terms of comprehensibility, manageability, and meaningfulness. It is not culturally bound, as sources of meaningfulness, how much information is comprehended, and what resources are applied to a given stressor may vary across cultures (Antonovsky 1996; Langeland and Vinje 2017).

Mental health from a salutogenic viewpoint pertains to understanding and enhancing adaptive capacities in people in order to promote a sense of coherence. Social support plays a key role in the promotion of coherence (Antonovsky 1979). The reciprocal relationship is that social support improves sense of coherence and sense of coherence allows a person to make use of social support. Instances when a person is not able to make use of social support suggest failures in epistemic trust. Impediments in epistemic trust interfere with salutogenesis and increase vulnerability to psychopathology (Fonagy *et al.* 2015). If there is an epistemic match, then patients can understand themselves better as the potential for influence is created. In the process, the patient regains capacity to be interested in the mental states of others and can learn from others. Art therapy helps recreate trust in the social world through experiential learning of how to be curious about self and others. It offers opportunities for epistemic matches and therefore promotes salutogenesis.

Developing resilience

There is growing research in support of a bi-factor model of mental health, which considers a spectrum of illness and general psychopathology more useful than traditional categorical conceptualizations, and recognizes a need for treatments—like mentalizing—with a transdiagnostic approach. Current research proposes that mental health disorders are explained by a general psychopathology dimension called the p factor (Bateman *et al.* 2018; Caspi *et al.* 2014; Patalay *et al.* 2015; Polek *et al.* 2018). For patients with a high p factor, there is an absence of expected resilience in the face of difficulties, lack of epistemic trust, and severe limitations in social learning and salutogenesis. They struggle to change because they cannot accept new information. In order to reach these patients, mentalizing is necessary, as it provides an environment conducive to reopening epistemic trust (Bateman *et al.* 2018). Mentalizing fosters "resilience in the face of stressful conditions, and the ability to take a different perspective as a result of adversity" (Bateman and Fonagy 2016, p.125). Similarly, art therapy is transdiagnostic and also creates conditions for the reopening of epistemic pathways, thereby building resilience. When people are enabled to use experiences of mentalizing to learn to mentalize others, they can then transfer these experiences to daily life (Bateman *et al.* 2018). We propose that patients may be more receptive to social communication transmitted through the artwork and its discussion. Art therapy opens the channel for knowledge transmission through its provision of ostensive signaling and mirroring opportunities, and recognition of each person as a subjective agentive self (Springham and Huet 2018). Art making can assist in regaining a sense of control, substituting avoidant and helpless behavior with more adaptive responses (Hass-Cohen and Findlay 2016). These processes build resilience.

Promoting agency and connection

Creating art promotes a sense of agency and control, as patients are fully in charge of what they create. They make choices and in so doing, become empowered as their sense of agency is recognized and fostered. The act of creating something out of nothing may also feel affirming and create a sense of mastery and self-esteem (Wadeson 2010). In art therapy, patients are called to purposeful action, creating a tangible art product to express their inner state and engaging in authorship by sharing personal meaning of the artwork (Greenwood 2012; Taylor-Buck and Havsteen-Franklin 2013). A Compass patient once expressed his wish to "feel life in his bones and in his blood." Recognition of the absence of such a purposeful and intentional existence incited his suicidal ideation and often led to feelings of hopelessness and despair. This patient engaged in art therapy and confirmed that he felt closest to living life intently when he was creating art. He spoke about having control of the image, stating, "I can make whatever I want. This [art] is my own thing. And that is very different from how I usually feel."

The artwork also helps to link one group member to another (Springham and Camic 2017). Some patients have "reduced capacity to keep themselves in mind or to recognize that others have them in mind when listening to the problems of others, which accounts, to some degree, for their anxiety about groups and their oscillations between over- and under-involvement with others" (Bateman and Fonagy 2016, p.156). In group therapy settings, patients can become involved in peers' issues and lose themselves in the process, leading to "rapid distancing from the other person to save themselves" (Bateman and Fonagy 2016, p.156). These intense responses toward and away from others demonstrate the interpersonal difficulties that sustain a sense of disconnection and loneliness experienced by young people with psychiatric issues. Mentalizing skills are necessary for people to practice functioning in dynamic and complex social situations. Group art therapy addresses the delicate balance between autonomy and connection, self and others. The artwork itself contributes a great deal toward that effort. For instance, art objects can aid in the process of containment and offer a physical representation of boundaries between internal worlds, because the art ultimately belongs to its creator. A patient who struggled with emotional boundaries described the artwork as a reminder for her to not take on others' issues as her own. When asked what that was like, the patient explained, "This is what I made and it goes in my folder. That is what you made and it goes in your folder. I can talk about your image, connect with it, have empathy for the emotions in it, but it does not belong to me. And you can do the same for my image, but it does not belong to you. I have a hard time remembering that."

We often ask patients to describe what they find helpful about the art therapy group. Usually, responses demonstrate the potential of art to draw people out from isolation.

One patient responded:

> I have a really hard time seeing how other people are feeling or what they're thinking, because I'm trapped in my mind. But, doing this I feel like I could really connect and understand what everybody said.

Another patient offered:

> I can see parts of myself, and what I have gone through, in most of the artwork from other people in this group. I thought at first that I couldn't really relate to my peers. I felt so different from everyone else. But when I look at the artwork, I can understand it and it makes me realize that what they were feeling is like what I feel. We have more in common than I thought we did.

The dialectic between autonomy and connectedness negotiated in the art therapy space parallels the central task of emerging adulthood, which we discuss in Chapter 4.

Encouraging empathy

Simon was a Compass patient who did not engage in therapeutic groups and often declined to attend. He acknowledged struggles with openness and vulnerability in groups, a tendency to participate superficially, and general avoidance of discussing salient issues. When present, he put his efforts toward distracting peers in the group. After several weeks of this behavior, a shift was noticed in an art therapy group where he created artwork about a place where he felt stuck. Simon drew himself as a stick figure sandwiched between two walls closing in. He spoke about feeling hopeless because his past was catching up to him and he was running out of space and time before the walls closed in. He said he had dug himself into a hole at school, procrastinating on schoolwork. His failing grades prevented him from transferring to a more desirable university, so he had to return to school in order to improve his grades first, even though he hated it there.

One peer likened his artwork to a grave because the figure was below the horizon line, subterranean. Upon hearing this, Simon became stoic and responded that the comment resonated with him. Another peer commented that the figure did not have a face and could not see that he was running from one wall into another. His peers also recognized a sense of urgency and imminent doom. Simon became tearful. He spoke about his struggle with suicidality for the first time. When the therapist checked in with him, asking about his experience in the group, Simon said he felt validated by peers. He acknowledged his avoidance in other groups, even earlier art therapy groups where he and his artwork were superficial. He said that he was forced to "see his feelings" and once he saw them, he had to feel them too. When the artwork was created, his emotions were externalized and he could interact with them differently. Simon added that even though it was difficult to show emotions in front of others, the group was a positive experience.

So how can Simon's experience of *seeing feelings* in his artwork be understood? Havsteen-Franklin (2016) highlights the four conceptual dimensions of mentalizing in relation to art therapy: affect consciousness, empathy, psychological mindedness, and mindfulness. Here, we focus on the affect consciousness and empathy dimensions, as they seem pertinent to Simon's experience in the group. First, the image created in art therapy was a way for Simon to communicate his affective state, embodied in the artwork. Embodied images transcend what is consciously known; they are more than mirrors of the inner state because they embody the internal state (Schaverien 1999). Simon's artwork prompted recognition of affect and communication of mental states that he skillfully worked to avoid. However, when these feelings were externalized, he was physically confronted with them. The art therapy process decreased Simon's experiential avoidance and increased his emotional awareness. Second, Simon's drawing seemed to rouse empathy, as his peers attempted to understand his experiences and offer their perspectives. The artwork provided material for group members to mutually attune to, explore, and validate. Simon often felt misunderstood because he was not able to show his authentic self to peers, taking on the role of the laid-back joker. Vulnerability in the group context was an unfamiliar experience for Simon, who recognized his reticence to verbally communicate feeling states. The physical art product seemed to provide an opening for Simon to empathize with himself and begin mentalizing his experiences.

Nonmentalizing
Nonmentalizing modes
To understand what mentalizing is, it is useful to learn what mentalizing is not. Bateman and Fonagy (2012a) identify three nonmentalizing modes: psychic equivalence, pretend mode, and teleological mode. These stances are also called prementalizing modes, because they are a part of natural development of mentalizing in children. They become problematic when adults revert to these modes when mentalizing capacity is diminished.

When we explain nonmentalizing to patients in the Compass Program, we steer clear of the specific jargon of prementalizing modes. Learning the nonmentalizing stances was extremely helpful for us because they serve as a guide to recognize what is happening in the patient and respond accordingly. For patients, it is not necessary to get into depth about the development of nonmentalizing modes; however, providing general information on what nonmentalizing looks like in group settings (e.g., giving advice, making assumptions without clarifying, intellectualizing, lack of curiosity, focusing on external factors, etc.) provides some structure. Here, we describe each nonmentalizing mode, providing examples of how they may present in art therapy.

Psychic equivalence: Feelings are equated to reality
In psychic equivalence mode, a person's internal world (feelings, thoughts, anything imagined) is experienced as real. This adds a

level of "drama as well as risk to interpersonal relationships, and patients' exaggerated emotional reactions are justified by the seriousness with which they suddenly experience their own and others' thoughts and feelings" (Allen *et al.* 2008, p.278). In Chapter 9, we describe the artwork of Stacy, a patient who frequently operated in psychic equivalence mode when in distress. In her artwork, Stacy drew a portrait of herself wielding a sword, defending herself from dragons. She felt attacked and therefore believed that others were out to get her. She, in turn, struck back accordingly. Her thinking supported psychic equivalence mode: I *feel* this way, so it *is* this way. Verfaille (2016) describes how patients may equate their inner experience with reality in art therapy, offering the example of a patient interpreting a disapproving look at their artwork as irrefutable proof that it is stupid and must be thrown away.

Pretend mode: Feelings are disconnected from reality

In pretend mode, a person's internal and external worlds are disconnected. They may speak at length, circularly, or use highly intellectualized language that does not link to genuine emotion (Allen *et al.* 2008; Bateman and Fonagy 2016). Patients whose artwork is disconnected from any emotion may be functioning in pretend mode. They may use eloquent speech to describe their artwork or focus on the aesthetic qualities, describing their work as if in an art class critique, though it may seem empty or lacking in emotional depth. On the other hand, they may create images that are emotionally provocative and then deny emotional connection to the image. (See, for example, the discussion in Chapter 5 about a patient's caterpillar and butterfly drawing.)

Teleological mode: Only what is observed in the physical world is reality

Patients operating in the prementalizing teleological mode tend to focus on external factors and actions, and may be extremely literal. Teleological reasoning is concrete, tending to center on goal-directed behavior instead of underlying thoughts, emotions, and motivations driving the behavior (Bateman and Fonagy 2016).

Havsteen-Franklin (2016) identified teleological mode in the way patients may frame the art therapy session, giving the example of a patient who viewed the art therapist as a teacher who could provide concrete art instruction yielding immediate results. In Chapter 8 we discuss the artwork of a patient depicting teleological structures of thinking because the identified solutions for his stuck place were external and action-focused (see also Figure 8.1).

How to address nonmentalizing

Nonmentalizing generates nonmentalizing. We have witnessed nonmentalizing spread like wildfire among groups of patients with personality disorders. As such, it is critical for therapists to intervene. Mentalizing therapists focus on helping patients regain their capacity to mentalize, instead of doing the work for the patient. It is important to recognize and stop nonmentalizing when it occurs, and offer judicious praise when patients are mentalizing well. Therapists must first identify the nonmentalizing mode the patient may be operating in, and then pause, rewind, and explore. Next, they intervene accordingly, with validation, transparency, and empathic challenging when appropriate (Bateman and Fonagy 2016).

Given the complexity of group art therapy, addressing nonmentalizing can be a rather difficult task. It is challenging to determine what to give priority to when time limitations prevent the ability to address every action and interaction between patients, therapists, and artwork. Early on, we fell into the trap of mentalizing *for* patients, offering suggestions, naming feelings, working hard to understand what was happening in the artwork of patients who offered no aid in this process. We found ourselves exhausted after each group. During a video conference meeting with our colleagues at ICAPT, they posed the question: *Why are you working harder than your patients are?* After that, it seemed so obvious. Their inquiry jolted us out of the pattern of meeting nonmentalizing from patients with our own mentalized responses, a practice that is not sustainable and ultimately leaves the patient's mentalizing problems unaddressed (Bateman and Fonagy 2016). Instead, the focus should be on calling attention to nonmentalizing and intervening in a way that gives the patients the opportunity to engage mentalizing. In well-functioning mentalizing groups, patients begin to help identify breaks in mentalizing and are invited to do so. They share responsibility for the mentalizing processes as they unfold, and are tasked with monitoring the group's mentalizing.

The following is a reconstruction of a discussion that took place in a rather difficult group with moments of nonmentalizing from both the patients and the art therapist. The group had had a few art therapy sessions previously, but cohesion was fragile at best. Amy, a patient with BPD, severe trauma, and suicidal ideation, had sporadic attendance due to being unit restricted for safety concerns and impulsivity. In this portion of the discussion, Amy shared an abstract painting created by layering various hues of blue and black watercolor.

> **Amy:** [*Showing her artwork*] I started with the watercolor layers. Usually I can keep my head above water but it feels like I'm drowning. The black started out as bubbles. But I kept dropping more and more water and it became this big dark thing. I guess I've been feeling overwhelmed and hopeless.
>
> **Bonnie:** It's beautiful!
>
> **Therapist:** Wait, wait. Let's try to stay away from blanket praise. Instead, can we speak more specifically? Bonnie, what is it that you find appealing about the image?
>
> **Bonnie:** All the layers are very vibrant.
>
> **Therapist:** Okay, you're responding to the bright layers. Thanks for clarifying.
>
> **Therapist:** [*To Amy*] And where would you be in the picture?
>
> **Amy:** I'd be beneath it. Off the page, drowning and blowing these bubbles up.
>
> **Bonnie:** But it's really pretty. I like the blue.

Kim: At least you're here getting help.

Joe: [*To therapist*] Can you fix my bracelet?

[*Joe takes off his beaded bracelet made in crafts and hands it to the therapist*]

Therapist: No, respect! Amy was talking.

Joe: But it broke.

Therapist: STOP. Wait a minute! [*Holding up hands*] Guys, what is happening here? Amy is talking about this really grave experience of feeling like she is underwater, drowning, and we're dumping compliments on her and focusing on other things. What's going on?

[*Silence*]

Here, the art therapist made an intentional effort to stop the action and call attention to what was happening in the group. One group member seemed focused on complimenting the image; another was distracted by something unrelated. The therapist holding up hands interrupted the nonmentalizing. At this point, the therapist also felt frustrated and confused by the group's evasiveness.

Therapist: What's that like for you, Amy?

Amy: [*Smiles, shrugs*]

Kim: Well, we don't have to be sad all the time.

Therapist: No, Kim, you don't have to be sad all the time. I imagine it would feel overwhelming to be sad all the time. But right now, this seems like it could be a sad experience for Amy and I wonder what it's like for her when we focus on what we like about the painting? Or avoid talking about it and ask me to fix bracelets instead?

Kim: I guess.

Amy: It's hard because I want to avoid it too. I'm smiling when I talk about it.

Bonnie: I smile too, but it's because I can relate to it, that feeling of being overwhelmed. I smile sometimes when things are serious.

Kim: I'm always smiling about serious things.

Therapist: Okay, so the smiles are coming from different places. Maybe some want to avoid the sad stuff. Others smile when talking about serious things. Where does that come from?

Joe: It's kind of a defense. To protect yourself, you know?

Bonnie: [*Nodding*]

Kim: [*Nodding*]

Therapist: I can see that. And what are the compliments and distractions about now? I don't know for sure, but could they be an effort to protect Amy? Or protect yourselves from something?

[*Silence*]

Kim: Let's go around and say positive affirmations.

Therapist: WAIT, WAIT A MINUTE! [*Holding up hands*] Some real, current difficulties have come up today. I'm not sure where the need to say positive affirmations is coming from, or if they would be helpful at this very moment. Maybe we can come back to it, but I'm still very curious about Amy's painting. Can we go back and try to mentalize about the image a bit more?

Kim: [*Rolling her eyes and sighing*] Fine.

Therapist: Kim, if YOU want to affirm yourself, go ahead.

Kim: [*Sighs*]

The therapist's frustration is evident here. There is a missed opportunity for the therapist to be curious about Kim's mind and motivation behind her request for affirmation, that is, "I'm curious about what makes you want to say affirmations" or "I notice you sighed and gave a look there. What's happening?" She seems to shut down afterward, and the therapist makes another attempt to re-engage, using transparency and self-disclosure.

Therapist: I think this is important work that you are all doing, and I want for us to give it space, to acknowledge it. This way of expressing and reflecting on our experiences can be powerful. I think it would be a disservice for us to be flippant or skirt over such important work. I'm feeling discouraged and I'm not sure about this, but it seems to me like that's happening right now. I wonder what that's about?

[Silence]

Therapist: Maybe it feels uncomfortable to talk about heavy feelings? Can we see if we can tolerate that a little better?

Bonnie: *[Nods]* Well, thank you for opening up to the group, Amy.

Joe: *[Nodding]* Yeah.

Amy: *[Smiling]* Well, the last time I acknowledged my true feelings, I got put on UR [unit restriction].

Amy shifts focus and seems to be joining the group here. Identifying a reason to not return to discussing her image, she instead discusses the staff's actions.

Therapist: What do you mean?

Amy: The other night I drew something that made the staff concerned, so they put me on UR.

Bonnie: Yeah, will you tell on us?

Joe: We can't draw what we really feel when there are consequences.

Therapist: Well you're right. I am a part of all the treatment teams and we do communicate with each other about what goes on in every group.

Amy: Well then, we can't express ourselves!

Kim: We'll get in trouble!

Therapist: Wait, let's pause here! A lot is taken into consideration for a person to be put on UR. Let's mentalize the staff a little bit. Why might they respond to an image, probably along with other factors, by putting someone on UR?

Amy: Well, they want to keep us safe. I understand that.

Bonnie: Yeah! That's like when I drew a blood waterfall with a smiley face next to it. People freaked out about it, but then I explained that the blood was keeping the smiley face happy, keeping it alive. We need blood to live.

Therapist: Oh. Sometimes the intention and the interpretation of an image can vary. Amy, was there a misinterpretation for your image? Did they not understand or think it meant something other than what you intended?

Amy: Nope. [*Smiling*] They got it right! But I didn't intend to make an image like that. It just came out of my subconscious or something. I don't understand.

Therapist: Yeah, it can feel confusing or surprising when we make something unexpected. What did you feel when you made your image?

Amy: It was kind of scary, I guess. It definitely scared my nurse!

Therapist: It's hard to balance expression with safety. We encourage you guys to express yourselves and it may feel like punishment for some people when the team responds to the artwork, usually along with other safety concerns, by putting you on UR. Really, safety is the priority in a hospital setting like this one.

Amy: I'm just glad I'm not on UR anymore.

Therapist: Me too. I'm glad you're feeling safer. And I wonder if there's a similar kind of scary feeling talking about your artwork now?

Amy: A little. I also don't want to bring other people down.

Therapist: Oh. Can we clarify with the group if they feel like your artwork is bringing them down? What do you guys think?

Bonnie: You're not bringing me down.

Kim: Well it's not happy, but it's good that you're talking about it.

Therapist: I also appreciate that you are talking about your artwork today. And I appreciate you guys sticking with it to try to understand Amy's experience a bit better. [*To group*] What would it feel like to be in Amy's image? If you were the figure off the page, drowning and blowing up these bubbles?

Kim: Terrifying. Hopeless.

Joe: It's like it's already over. Like you're already at the bottom, so why try?

Bonnie: But maybe the bubbles mean there is still hope. The person is still alive if they're blowing up bubbles.

Therapist: It brings up several questions for me, too, like how did the figure get all the way to the bottom, off the page? What makes it hard to stay afloat? What would be happening on the surface of the water? Amy, any response to what peers said? Did anything seem to fit for you or your experience?

Amy: The hopelessness. I've been stuck there lately and I'm not sure how to come out of it.

This discussion unfolded in a matter of minutes, demonstrating the complexity of fast-pace group interactions in art therapy. The group had difficulty staying with the image, but after several attempts to bring them back, they began to explore the artwork productively, focus on the affect, and attune to Amy's experience.

Another group struggled to respond to a member, Carol, who was the self-proclaimed worst patient with the most difficult and unique struggles. Group members initially met these claims with silence, presumably fearful of Carol's volatility, which further isolated her. Later, with time and some transparency on Carol's part, they were able to begin challenging the fatalistic certainty she brought with her to the group. The following reconstruction of discussions in the art therapy group and individually with the art therapist captures Carol's progression, characterized by gradual shifts in her ability to share her mind with others.

> **Group member #1:** Let's talk about Carol's drawing next.

> **Carol:** I have an issue with agency. I don't have a very strong sense of self and I limit all of my goals and wants and I turn everything into a prison—my environment, relationships, those are the things that trap me. So I drew the milieu and I feel like I am in physical prison because I literally can't get out. The doors are locked here. Also, I get put on UR [unit restriction] a lot and that kills me and makes me feel really trapped at Menninger. I drew barbed wire and chains and tally marks. I do use tally marks to count the days. It helps me feel like I'm actually accomplishing something. I'm trapped here in this present moment where I'm not accomplishing anything. I'm not in school, don't have a job, and don't have any friends. I don't have my parents because they don't really want me; they sent me here. I don't have any motivation to do anything. I'm better off dead than being here. This is week nine for me. I'm supposed to be looking at aftercare options, I'm supposed to know what I want to do with my life, but I just don't want it. So I really am stuck here.

> [*Silence*]

> **Therapist:** I have some thoughts but I'm curious what is it like for you guys to hear Carol and see this part of her experience in her drawing? How are you responding to the artwork?

[*Silence*]

Group member #2: I want to empathize but it's really difficult for me. It feels hard to relate, so I'm trying to find ways to try to feel what you're feeling in that situation. I understand what it's like to have a lack of motivation but I don't think I've ever felt wholly unmotivated and completely hopeless about the world. That's something I've been able to hold on to, so to try to think of what it would feel like to not have any of that is very difficult for me, but I imagine it would feel very painful.

[*Prolonged silence*] Carol stares blankly at Member #2. One group member looks out the window; another looks toward the door; and a few more look down at their own artwork—all seem to avoid Carol's gaze.

Therapist: There's something about what you said [*to Member #2*] and what you said Carol that feels absolute to me, very certain. You said "completely" and you're talking about a total lack of motivation and will, to live even. For me, hearing you speak with such certainty is hard to hear. And it seems extremely difficult to live it. About the image, I'm noticing how the barbed wire is inside the building. I'm so curious about that.

Carol: It's just a metaphor!

Therapist: I understand that, but I see the brick on the outside—

Carol: [*Interrupting abruptly, rolling her eyes and raising her voice*] That's a very literal brick! We have brick on the outside of the terrace.

At this point a group member physically leans back into his chair, distancing himself from the table. Others seem to freeze at Carol's irritability, looking at the art therapist with wide, searching eyes.

Therapist: Yes, I know we have brick outside the terrace. I'm sensing a little combativeness from you and I'm uncertain about where that might be coming from? Or if I am mis-interpreting your response to me?

Carol: It's nothing specific.

Therapist: Well I was going to say something about the internal/ external space. When I look at the barbed wire metaphor inside of the building, I think of how we keep ourselves stuck. Those internal limitations in addition to the exterior/physical barriers of the space really would create a trapped feeling on two fronts, from the outside and the inside.

[*Silence*]

Therapist: What would you title your piece if you were to give it one?

Carol: "Mennin-gitis."

[*Group laughter*]

Prolonged silences reflect nonmentalizing and are problematic, as the mentalizing stance values active group facilitation (Allen and Fonagy 2006). For people with personality disorders, an unresponsive therapist is harmful, as patients may interpret the silence as judgment and criticism from an authority figure (Springham *et al.* 2012). This is iatrogenic and may cause re-experiencing of painful attachment injuries. In this case the silences were also problematic when they were filled with the therapist sharing her perception instead of calling attention to the silences. Questions like, *I'm noticing a lot of silence and I wonder what that is about? What's happening in these silences?* would help to orient the group to the present moment.

Additionally, lack of transparency, inattention to affect, and disregard for nonverbal cues reflect nonmentalizing. Carol's shift in tone of voice signaled that something may be happening internally. The group's nonverbal cues and physical withdrawal from Carol's image suggested unstated emotional reactions. Verbal recognition of these cues may have invited Carol and peers to be transparent about feelings in the moment. Open questions about affective states may have helped to make those automatic responses more explicit or to incite reflection. Bateman and Fonagy (2016, p.255) note that affect focus is the "elephant in the room" and the "aspect of implicit mentalizing that is influencing the interaction but is hidden and unstated." Instead of calling attention to the patient's combativeness, the therapist might have shared her own feeling of discomfort about palpable distress in the room. This would have been a more mentalizing response as it demonstrates transparency and affect focus.

When Carol responded abruptly, with "It's just a metaphor!" the therapist immediately jumped in to defend herself. The "I understand, but—" stance is not usually helpful for mentalizing. There was a lack of explicit validation for Carol's emotions and more focus on clarifying the therapist's intention. An important aspect of mentalizing work is the acknowledgment that nonmentalizing happens in both patient and therapist, and that opportunities for repairing these lapses surface frequently. The resurfacing of ruptures may seem problematic but is actually beneficial for patients with attachment trauma as it is reparative and offers a model for healthy attachment relationships, which are inevitably flawed.

Immediately after the group, the art therapist followed up with Carol individually. There was some recognition of the art therapist's contributions to problems in the group and an attempt at repair.

Therapist: Did you understand what I was asking you in the group?

Carol: You asked a lot of things.

Therapist: I did. It was when I used the word "combative."

Carol: Yeah.

Therapist: That was not the best choice of words on my part. I was taken aback by your response and it occurs to me now that you may have been feeling attacked, or something like that. If I said something that made you feel that way, I want to apologize and see if we can try to understand what happened.

Carol: I just thought it was stupid. I was self-conscious and hated what I drew, so I just wanted to listen when we discussed and then I didn't. I ended up sharing for some reason.

Therapist: I had no idea you were feeling so critical of your own drawing. Does that happen a lot in art therapy or is it today, specifically?

Carol: I don't know.

Therapist: Oh. I am sorry. I apologize if what I said came off as critical. I was trying to communicate that I felt the stuckness you depicted in your drawing, actually.

Carol: I regret sharing. It was really invalidating.

Therapist: In what way?

Carol: I should've known that no one feels the way I do. No one is ever as sad as I am, like inhumanly sad [*crying*]. I'm impossible. Nobody can empathize with me.

Therapist: I really didn't know you were feeling this way. I also hear a lot of extremes in what you're saying and the intensity of your emotions.

Carol: There were ten people in that group and only two spoke. Including you, the leader, and so only one peer responded to it.

Therapist: And what does that mean to you?

Carol: They couldn't connect. No one can. It's why I'm alone.

Therapist: Hmmm. So you didn't hear from more people in the group and that made you feel alone?

Carol: Yes!

Therapist: I can see how it would feel that way. I'm also thinking of the theme, the idea of where or how you feel stuck. I believe that your image was different than your peers' in some ways. You created the physical place of treatment and their images were a bit more abstract, about issues they struggle with. But the fact that everyone responded to that prompt at all means that we all have places of stuckness. And maybe I'm trying to assuage a little right now, but there is some commonality in that.

Carol: They're stuck with things that I don't have. My only feedback was you saying what I said in different terms and another peer telling me that she can't empathize with such little hope/no hope. I didn't spark anything from anyone else, not even any questions. I wish I hadn't shared.

Therapist: I'm so sorry, Carol. I didn't grasp that you felt disconnected in the moment when it was happening in the group. And I can see how that could pile on to the tough day you've been having. What would it be like to say what's happening? To tell us when you feel self-critical or attacked or disconnected?

Carol: I don't know.

Therapist: I don't know either. But maybe you can give it a try next time. It would at least help me understand better what's going on.

[*Silence*]

Therapist: I will see you next time then? I hope this is not something that will prevent you from returning to the group in the future.

Carol: Yeah, I don't think I'm going to go anymore.

Therapist: I would like for you to come back, but if you choose not to go, would it be okay if I—

Carol: [*Interrupting*] You want to give someone else my spot in the group? Go ahead! Is it [*states another patient's name*]? I think the group would be happy to have her instead of me in there!

Therapist: No. Actually, that's not what I was going to say at all. I wanted to see if you'd be okay with me checking in next week before the group to see what your stance is on returning then.

I was also going to ask if you'd like to try individual art therapy in the meantime. I do think there is some value in your visual exploration of these topics for the time being, until you decide to return to the group. But I'm so curious, Carol, what made you think I wanted to give your spot away to someone else?

Carol: I don't know. It's pointless anyway.

Therapist: I don't want to push you into doing anything you're choosing not to do, but I would encourage you to think on it. Your spot is yours and it will be there for you when you're ready. I'm going to check in on you anyway next week to see where you're at on returning, okay?

Carol: Okay.

Carol returned the following week and had a similar abrupt interaction with a peer. This time, she was able to be a little more transparent about her internal state.

Carol: My image is about things that have helped other people that are not able to help me. I'm completely hopeless. Nothing works for me.

Group member #2: It's so hard to respond. It's like you're so certain that everything is bad. I feel as stuck as you say you are when I hear you explain your artwork.

Group member #3: I agree. It's like there is no room for anything but hopelessness.

Everett: I'm having a different response. I'm drawn to the bright colors in the image. It makes me think that even though you say nothing has worked, you are here, in this group, trying. I'm thinking that means there is still a little hope, if only a sliver.

Carol: I'm worse off than anyone else here. I don't have hope. I don't even want hope here, in this place where I'm stuck that feels like a prison. I'd rather be dead. How can I find hope somewhere that I'm trapped?

Everett: I'm just saying that maybe there's space for a little hope.

Carol: No! [*Abruptly, snapping at Everett*]

[*Silence*]

Therapist: What just happened here? I heard an attempt from Everett to offer his perspective, and then I heard a very curt response. Carol, how did you understand what he said?

Carol: I feel judged! Like it's my fault I'm hopeless.

Everett: I wasn't judging you. When I looked at the bright colors in the image and some open space, I saw a bit of hope.

Therapist: Carol, your reaction makes a bit more sense to me now, actually. I thought it was out of the blue, but I'm hearing and seeing that you get a bit snappy when you feel judged, maybe even attacked?

Carol: Yeah.

Therapist: I can see that. And I'm also hearing from Everett that that wasn't his intention.

Everett: No. I don't want Carol to be offended. I didn't mean to sound judgmental. I just came in here with a really positive attitude today, and I realize that might not be the place she's in. This is a new experience for me to feel this way, to feel some happiness and hope. Sorry if I was pushing it on you, Carol.

Carol: No, I'm sorry too. My perception is really warped sometimes. I see things that aren't there and it's a problem.

Therapist: Both of you are really starting to mentalize here. Nice work! I appreciate when you're open about what you're bringing with you to group, and thinking about how that impacts the way you interact with each other, and clarifying your thoughts and feelings. How does that feel?

Carol: Fine.

Everett: I felt bad sitting here thinking that I upset Carol but now it helps that we know where we're both coming from.

After this clarification, Carol was able to regulate her emotions and the group could return to the other comments about her image. She tolerated peers' recognition of absolute certainty present in her speech. Peers began to challenge Carol's certainty with some hesitance, as there was still a fear that she would respond with volatility. The art therapy group seemed to be one of the few contexts where Carol could tolerate any confrontation, and also where peers were able to confront her. They were talking about the artwork, not the patient directly, so it is likely that distance provided an opportunity to challenge nonmentalizing.

CHAPTER 3

Menninger, Art Therapy, and the Compass Program

Here, we provide a description of The Menninger Clinic and the Compass Program to offer context for the MBAT group and interventions described in the chapters that follow. First, we review the history and development of art therapy at The Menninger Clinic. Next, we offer an overview of the Compass patient, with background information and diagnostic makeup. Finally, we detail the Compass Program structure, including mentalizing-based groups offered to patients.

Development of art therapy at The Menninger Clinic

Art therapy has a robust history at The Menninger Clinic. Before the development of art therapy as a distinct field, art was offered to Menninger patients in Topeka, Kansas. The Menningers believed art could help patients recover, and encouraged the development of activity therapies (Junge 1994; Malchiodi 2007). The history of art therapy at Menninger cannot be told without Mary Huntoon as its original champion, the central figure. Wix (2000) described Huntoon as the forgotten Midwestern counterpart to her better-known eastern colleagues, Edith Kramer, Margaret Naumburg, and Florence Cane. Mary Huntoon was an artist, art educator, and art therapist. Her early contributions to the art therapy field have garnered recognition (Junge 1994; Wix 2000, 2017). As a trained artist, Huntoon used art as therapy in the 1930s in her work with psychiatric patients, offering studio art to her "student" patients in order to provide a means for healing and self-expression. Huntoon guided patients through her use of art to meet their needs and goals. Following Huntoon, Don Jones and Robert Ault provided art therapy in the 1950s and 1960s. Both made a valuable impact and contributions to the field of art therapy in the United States (Junge 1994; Malchiodi 2007). Over time, the role of art therapy at Menninger has expanded and contracted, waxed and waned, but we are happy to report that it is ever-present. With reverence for those who came before, we are honored to continue their legacy.

Currently, art therapy is subsumed under psychiatric rehabilitation services, formerly activities therapy. Within the psychiatric rehabilitation model, professionals from various backgrounds work with patients to assess and improve functioning in living, working, academic, and social environments of their choice (Pratt *et al.* 2014). Psychiatric rehabilitation specialists facilitate many of the groups made available to patients at The Menninger Clinic, in addition to individual consultations in expressive therapies, social functioning, and vocational counseling, according to specific areas of training and expertise. As the rehabilitation specialist for the Compass Program is also an art therapist, Compass patients are uniquely positioned to experience creative approaches to mentalizing. Patients have access to various expressive interventions designed to promote mentalizing.

Art therapy is used with different populations in a number of human service organizations where art therapists take on various roles (Rubin 2011). Resultantly, art therapists have developed agility unlike many other professions, contorting to fit the structure and needs of their hiring organizations. While art therapy has a rich history at Menninger, it has, over time, been relegated to the confines of a discipline that at best grazes the surface of its potential for rich clinical understanding of the patients who engage it.

At least, we seemed to share that sentiment when we began our work at the hospital. It was difficult to find our footing and to make others understand where art therapy fit into the aims and structure of treatment. This is no new obstacle, as many art therapists have to provide education to other disciplines and administrators who unknowingly put art therapy into small mislabeled boxes, placed on the same shelf as craft time and other recreational activities. For us, this frustration is mitigated by the mentalizing approach. The mentalizing framework unlocks possibilities and offers liberty for art therapists to creatively address the aims of treatment. MBT aligns with art therapy quite seamlessly. In the Compass Program, mentalizing has unearthed some of art therapy's potential, and art therapy has enhanced the mentalizing capacity of patients, specifically with the provision of visual artifacts of the patient's experience that can be examined and explored. MBAT has enriched the depth of understanding for both patients and clinicians.

Overview of the Compass Program for Young Adults

The Compass Program for Young Adults was developed at The Menninger Clinic in the late 1990s to treat young people, ages 18 to 30. Emerging adult patients were previously admitted to traditional adult units at the hospital. The Compass Program came to inception when clinicians recognized the unique developmental difficulties inherent in this phase of life. Early adult patients had difficulty relating to an older adult treatment milieu and were not appropriate for an adolescent unit; thus, the Compass Program was established (O'Malley 2018). In the Compass Program, the aim of treatment is to provide assistance for emerging adults struggling to manage the transition from adolescence to adulthood in the face of complex psychiatric difficulties. The Program includes patients with a variety of treatment issues including anxiety, addiction, mood disorders, self-harm behavior, suicidal behavior, self-esteem issues, gender identity, or sexual issues (The Menninger Clinic 2014). Emerging adults also face challenges associated with developing identities and difficulties in interpersonal relationships (Arnett 2007). This is further complicated by personality disorders, which are prevalent among Compass patients and established in this phase of life.

Patients enter the Compass unit with many things in tow, tangible and intangible. Luggage carts roll in, lined with belongings, necessities, and comforts. In addition to these visible items, they also bring with them things we cannot see: experiences of anxiety, depression, trauma histories; debilitating lack of success with previous treatments; anger and resentment about coercion tactics used by parents to achieve their voluntary admission; skepticism about treatment providers' intentions and ability to help. The work of mentalizing is making the unseen visible, bringing these doubts, fears, and feelings to light, and making the implicit explicit. Mentalizing is used throughout the treatment process as the organizing scaffolding for patients and clinicians.

Patients enter the Program for treatment, diagnostic formulation, and recommendations for future treatment. The average length of stay for patients in the Compass Program is six to eight weeks (The Menninger Clinic 2014), approximately 49.2 days. Many patients are recommended for additional support following hospitalization, often entailing residential treatment with an emphasis on community re-integration.

Profile of a Compass patient

The research team at The Menninger Clinic provided the following demographic data from 2012 to 2018, collected from outcome measures administered upon admission to the Compass Program. Compass is a specialty psychiatric hospital program with no shortage of resources (O'Malley 2018; Poa 2006). Our emerging adult patients typically belong to families with high socioeconomic standing. Compass consists of primarily Caucasian patients (88.2%) with some college education (61.5%), many on leave from school to seek treatment.

Upon admission, the research team administers a number of questionnaires (see Figure 3.1) and assessments, including the Structured Clinical Interview for DSM-IV (SCID) (*Diagnostic and Statistical Manual of Mental Disorders*, Fourth edition) (First and

Spitzer 1997).[1] These diagnostic tools provide initial impressions that are refined over the course of treatment leading up to the diagnostic conference. Initial impressions are like an image that is out of focus. As patients engage in treatment processes and the team comes to know them better, the image sharpens, providing a clearer, crisper picture. The diagnostic process helps to hone that image. Sometimes it comes into high focus, and sometimes parts of the image remain blurry.

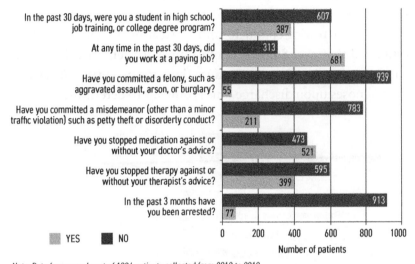

Note: Data from sample set of 1004 patients collected from 2012 to 2018.

Figure 3.1. Admission questions

---

1   The DSM-IV categorizes mental health disorders using a multi-axial system: Axis I includes any mental health conditions other than personality disorders or mental retardation (changed to intellectual developmental disorder in the DSM-5); Axis II includes personality and developmental disorders. Although the data in the book is from DSM-IV, Menninger has since shifted to using DSM-5, which no longer makes these distinctions (APA (American Psychiatric Association) 2000, 2013).

Figure 3.2 depicts Compass patients' difficulties with depression, anxiety, substance and alcohol dependence, and trauma. Of the personality disorders endorsed from the SCID, borderline personality disorder (BPD), avoidant personality disorder (APD), and obsessive-compulsive personality disorder (OCPD) prevail (see Figure 3.3). This data is based solely on patient reports early in treatment during a structured interview. It represents a total of 1004 patients, most of whom have co-occurring diagnoses. The SCID is part of the diagnostic formulation, but these numbers usually increase with observations and input from treatment team members and psychological testing conducted during treatment. One psychiatrist estimated that over 80 percent of Compass patients are diagnosed with a personality disorder. Because there are no current measures for diagnoses upon discharge, this is difficult to determine.

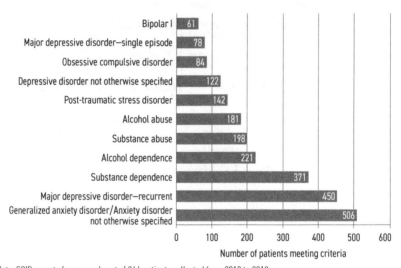

Note: SCID reports from sample set of 964 patients collected from 2012 to 2018.

Figure 3.2. Axis I diagnoses

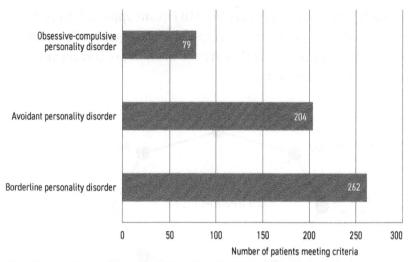

Note: SCID reports from sample set of 962 patients collected from 2012 to 2018.

Figure 3.3. Axis II diagnoses

The Compass treatment team

A multidisciplinary approach to treatment is integral to comprehensive understanding of each patient. At The Menninger Clinic, mental health professionals from various backgrounds work together on a treatment team. This includes a psychiatrist, psychologist, rehabilitation specialist, social worker, nursing staff, and an addictions counselor, or eating disorder specialist when warranted (see Figure 3.4). While individual therapists are not included in the core treatment team, they occupy key roles in the treatment process. Individual therapists do not typically participate in team rounds or meetings, but they maintain communication with team members about how patients are progressing. There is intention behind keeping this relationship protected, to ensure that patients feel secure and to promote a therapeutic alliance. Team members use their unique perspectives to conceptualize the patient and formulate a diagnostic narrative (Allen, Bleiberg and Haslam-Hopwood 2003; The Menninger Clinic 2014). The inclusion of multiple perspectives is essential for well-rounded evaluation of each patient and supports the MBT team approach to patients who are difficult to treat. We emphasize the agency of patients in the treatment process, as they are the most important members of the core treatment team.

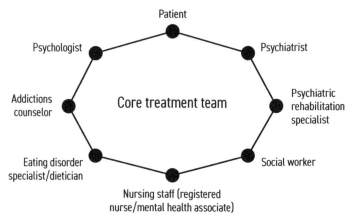

Figure 3.4. Core treatment team

The Compass Program structure

Treatment includes medication, individual psychotherapy, group psychotherapy, educational and experiential groups, family therapy, and therapeutic leisure activities within a community. Individual and group work with addictions counselors and eating disorder specialists are also available for patients struggling with these issues. The social environment provided by milieu therapy offers support, community, and learning opportunities with peers. Mentalizing is woven throughout treatment and serves as a compass, guiding providers from various treatment backgrounds and orientations (Allen *et al.* 2003; O'Malley 2018).

Creative group interventions that foster mentalizing

In addition to the general stance of the program, mentalizing is explicitly practiced in several key groups where creative interventions are present: Mentalizing, Creative Expressions, Social Skills and

Role-Play, and MBAT. Patients are made aware of the mentalizing focus in each of these groups, which meet once per week. The MBAT group is discussed in detail throughout subsequent chapters (Chapters 5–8). Here, we provide a brief description of the other mentalizing-focused groups offered to Compass patients.

Mentalizing group

In the Compass Program, patients receive mentalizing education in the group context. The therapists explain that mentalizing will permeate their treatment, as it is the foundation for the Compass Program. The Mentalizing group meets at the beginning of each week to review topics related to mentalizing and provides exercises to promote mentalizing. Upon arrival to the group, patients receive a handout (see Figure 3.5) outlining the basics of mentalizing. Over time, the Mentalizing group has adapted to include interactive activities demonstrative of mentalizing processes because the young adult population calls for more dynamic learning experiences in addition to psychoeducation, with tasks to promote and illustrate mentalizing (Tobias *et al.* 2006). The *Handbook of Mentalizing in Mental Health Practice* describes a number of experiential exercises used in the Mentalizing group (see Allen *et al.* 2012). Concurrently, in the treatment milieu, staff work to create a culture of mentalizing in interactions among staff and patients. Patients are encouraged to continue a mentalizing stance in peer-to-peer interactions. Therapists and treatment providers from all disciplines model and promote mentalizing in therapy sessions with patients (O'Malley 2018).

What?

	Self	Other(s)
Thoughts		
Feelings		
Behavior		

- Being aware and curious about the thoughts and feelings of self and others.

- Thinking about thoughts, feelings, and experiences that underlie behaviors in self and others.

- Attending to states of mind in oneself and others.

- Understanding misunderstandings.

Mentalizing tells us not to assume that we can attach a specific meaning to behavior, without looking into it further and trying to understand the other possible motivations behind it.

This includes both the way we perceive the reasons for the behavior of others, and the way we interpret the reasons for our own behavior.

Why?

- Mentalizing => understanding.

- Fosters secure attachment relationships with self and others.

- Key to self-regulation and self-direction.

- Exercise the mentalizing muscle.

- Practice mentalizing because it's most difficult to do when it's most needed—increase in emotional arousal => decrease in ability to mentalize.

- People are often quick to assign meaning to behavior, without actually knowing whether it is accurate.

- The process of pausing to think sets aside hasty assumptions and allows for consideration of alternative motivations for behaviors.

- To promote mental flexibility, get out of fixed and rigid ways of thinking.

- To make informed decisions based on mentalizing (vs. impulsivity, reactivity).

- Helps develop a sense of self that is cohesive, continuous, and responsible for our choices and behavior.

How?

Transparency
- Explicitly stating own thoughts and feelings
- Allowing for an open understanding of thoughts and feelings of self and others

Attitude of not knowing
- Flexible/open mindset
- Respect the opacity of the mind

Curious stance
- Clarify assumptions (I wonder, I'm curious about, help me understand...)
- Questioning initial thoughts and feelings to consider what may be beneath the surface

Pause button
- Stopping the action; slowing down to allow for time and space to reflect
- Used to stop and think

- Sit with feelings— acknowledging and accepting difficult emotions without acting on them.

- Reflect vs. react.

- Clarify ASSUMPTIONS.

- No ABSOLUTE CERTAINTY. Red flags for nonmentalizing: always, only, never, just, etc.

Mentalizing process:
Notice what's happening → pause button → reflect vs. react → sit with feelings → clarify assumptions → make decisions based on mentalizing.

Figure 3.5. Mentalizing

Creative Expressions group

Creative Expressions employs art, music, movement, and writing to provide mentalizing experiences for patients to engage. Unlike art therapy, which is a referral group, this group is open to all emerging adults on Compass. While some immediately express repulsion to arts-based modalities, it can be an enjoyable experience for many of the patients. They are encouraged to use mental flexibility to engage in unfamiliar and potentially uncomfortable activities. Emotions experienced in the milieu can also impact patient participation. When the patients feel connected to their peers and milieu cohesion and support are present, they tend to approach this group with expressive freedom.

A number of the group activities are inspired by psychodrama interventions, which provide opportunities for patients to consider thoughts and feelings of self and others (Dayton 1994; Moreno and Moreno 1969). One group activity invites patients to create a group sculpture (Dayton 1994), by moving around the room and posing in a position that represents current thoughts and feelings about treatment. During this exercise, group members are observed slumped over in chairs, lying on the floor in fetal position, gazing longingly out the window, confidently poised standing on chairs, and sitting with arms outstretched. Some patients choose to leave the room. Group members are encouraged to be curious about each other's position, asking questions, identifying feelings elicited from each pose, and considering how the poses align with that patient's perceptions.

Social Skills and Role-Play group

The Social Skills and Role-Play group is framed for patients as a mentalizing workshop, with emphasis on using role-play to mentalize relationships. Psychodrama, which naturally encourages mentalizing, inspires the Role-Play group. The role-play may be anticipatory, or patients can use the group to reflect on past interactions. One goal of this group is to promote the patient's awareness of the other's perspective. Patients provide personal examples of relationship conflicts, misunderstandings, and curiosities, with families, friends, treatment providers, and peers in the milieu. The patient who is role-playing has a live audience of peers as mentalizing is practiced. Patients receive feedback on their application of various social skills as their peers identify specific moments in the role-play when mentalizing was utilized well, and areas for improvement. The patient also joins the group members in processing reactions to the role-play.

Patients are also asked to play different roles. When the patient is in the role of a parent, sibling, or treatment team member, they are required to consider another's thoughts, feelings, and motivations. Napier and Chesner (2014) describe mentalizing in psychodrama as responding to the recent past "as if" it is in the present. Role reversal offers concretized perspective shifting as the patient interacts with self from the outside. Group members are able to consider alternative perspectives and shift awareness. The patient and group members have access to mental states of those involved in the role-play, with more immediacy than a verbal narrative (Dayton 2005; Moreno and Moreno 1969). For example, a patient struggling with the idea of continued residential treatment following hospitalization was asked to play the role of his parent. During role-play he was able to identify and consider the thoughts and emotions driving his parents' wishes for his continued treatment. "Your father and I are worried about you," the patient stated, while playing the role of his mother. "That suicide attempt terrified and devastated us. We want for you to be safe. We want to make sure we do everything we can to prevent this from happening again." The patient was able to pause and consider that his parents may be motivated by more than a need to control or "take over" his life, as was his previous position.

The playful nature of the role-play calls for creativity and motivates flexible thinking. Laughter frequently fills the room during this group, as patients are permitted and encouraged to "play" in various roles. Playfulness can prepare patients for serious work, though at times the group elects to stay in the play, and patients are reluctant to address more salient issues. Balancing the playfulness and monitoring mentalizing is the work of the therapist. It is also necessary to recognize nonmentalizing and to stop it abruptly (Allen *et al.* 2008). Pausing the role-play, explicitly expressing curiosity about what is happening, acknowledging experiential avoidance, and inviting group members to identify nonmentalizing can accomplish this task. These interventions also invite patients to claim responsibility and take agency for mentalizing processes as they unfold in the group.

CHAPTER 4

Emerging Adulthood, Mentalizing, and Art Therapy

Setting the emerging adult stage

The emerging adulthood stage was proposed by Jeffrey Arnett to define and distinguish the unique developmental period from ages 18 to 25 for young people in industrialized societies (Arnett 2000a, 2004). Arnett differentiates emerging adulthood from young adulthood, as adulthood has not yet been reached during this time, and young adulthood does not sufficiently define the period. Furthermore, the word *emerging* captures the fluidity of the period. Although Arnett (2000a, 2004) initially focuses on ages 18–25 as a rough indicator of the transition from emerging adulthood to young adulthood, Arnett, Zukauskiene, and Sugimura (2014) later broaden the age limit to 29. Here, we use the term broadly to include all the patients in the Compass Program whose ages range from 18 to 30, although the average age on Compass is 21.9 years. We use the term *emerging adult* interchangeably with the term *young adult*, as the Compass Program is comprised of both.

Making a case for new theories of human development, supporters of Arnett assert that previous theories no longer reflect the current experiences of people in modern society. Despite their seminal contributions to developmental psychology, Freud, Piaget, Erikson, and Havighurst are counted among the ranks of outdated theorists because the premise of entry into stable adult, gender-specific and heteronormative roles no longer holds up for young people in 21st-century industrialized societies (Arnett *et al.* 2011). The existence of a new emerging adult stage provides a foundation for explanation of the changing development of young people.

While many agree that emerging adulthood captures changes that were not accounted for or did not exist in previous conceptualizations of the trajectory into adulthood (Vespa 2017), a debate on the value of the stage model has transpired. Critics consider that a stage model does not explain the mechanisms of change in human behavior, but merely describes them. They also argue that stages do little to clarify or capture individual transitions, or to account for people who deviate. Opponents contend that a stage model fails to account for the nuance of this time period, and varied experiences across culture, geographic location, and socioeconomic factors. Overall, culturally based life stages lack universality and are only applicable to "small groups of people at certain historical times within certain societies" (Arnett *et al.* 2011, p.7; see also Hendry and Kloep 2007).

Despite the criticisms about the value of using a stage model to define this period, a general consensus exists that it is different than other periods of development. Even opponents concede the importance of Arnett's widespread distribution of his observations on emerging adulthood, as they have generated inquiry and have implications for education, health, and public policy. Both critics and supporters of the emerging adulthood stage theory agree that it is not a theory for all time; as cultures evolve and transform, so must the frameworks used for understanding the people within them (Arnett *et al.* 2011). We believe that the emerging adulthood period merits observation and description, as it offers a useful way of understanding young people in this time. The emerging adult stage theory fosters an appreciation for the unique struggles of our patients, almost all of whom fit within the demographic of western, developed, industrialized society. The Compass Program was founded and currently operates under the belief that emerging adulthood is distinct, and the developmental tasks of this period include addressing the conflicts revolving around independence and autonomy with simultaneous support from parents and societal structures (O'Malley 2018; Poa 2006).

Development of the emerging adult stage

The development of the emerging adult stage model can be credited largely to shifts in demographics, from changes in the age of marriage and childbirth and the rise in people obtaining higher education. These shifts have altered the course of development for many young people in the United States and other industrialized countries (Arnett 2000a; Vespa 2017). Delayed marriage and parenthood contribute to the unpredictability of this period. Emerging adulthood is widely variable due to less strict role requirements. Residential status, for example, is varied and unstable. School attendance is also diverse among emerging adults. This variability reflects the transitional nature of emerging adulthood and its focus on exploration and change. This period has shifted away from being a time for young people to settle down into marriage, parenthood, long-term residence, and stable career roles. Instead, it is marked with exploring various possibilities as young adults try out new roles.

Variability in emerging adulthood distinguishes it from other periods. According to Arnett, emerging adulthood is different from adolescence and adulthood due to relative independence from social responsibilities and expectations. Caught in-between the more dependent roles of adolescence and not yet immersed in the obligations of adulthood, emerging adults have more freedom for exploration. It is a time when multiple directions are possible and uncertainty abounds. The scope of options is greater for most people during emerging adulthood than at any other life period (Arnett 2000a). Yet, the freedom to choose from and explore these options may be limited by socioeconomic, cultural, or psychological realities. As previously discussed, Arnett acknowledges that the emerging adulthood period is a cultural construct and therefore not universal (2000a). This period is described as distinctive and also heterogeneous, complex, and dynamic (Arnett *et al.* 2011). In fact, the heterogeneity of emerging adulthood is essential to understanding it. The freedom from social control and strict norms during this time allows for diversity and a wide range of individual differences (Arnett 2006).

Key features of emerging adulthood

Five key features characterize emerging adulthood: the age of identity exploration, of instability, of self-focus, of feeling in-between, and of possibilities (Arnett 2004). In the same vein as Arnett *et al*.'s (2014) examination of the key features of emerging adulthood and their mental health implications, we describe them in terms of how they directly relate to Compass patients at The Menninger Clinic, providing examples of artwork representing each feature.

Age of identity exploration

Previously conceived as a task of adolescence, identity exploration occurs in emerging adulthood as young people explore possibilities in various areas of life, including love, work, and worldviews (Arnett 2004, 2006). By making decisions about romantic relationships, vocation, values, and beliefs, young people are responding to the question: *Who am I?* As they learn what kind of person they want to commit to, what kind of work they are suited for, what kind of worldview they will form, they are learning about who they are and consolidating their identity. When problems in identity explorations present, young adults experience confusion and are not able to make choices about relationships, meaningful roles, or worldviews; or they may feel that choices are out of reach (Arnett *et al*. 2014).

Mental health implications for identity exploration are vast. According to the American Psychiatric Association (APA 2013), identity disturbance is present in several DSM diagnoses, including BPD. A subgroup of Compass patients is made up of young adults who have been unsuccessful at navigating the transition from adolescence to adulthood. Stuck in adolescence, lacking in maturation, and unable to gain a sense of self-identity or independence from families, these young people fail to complete the task of individuation (Poa 2006). Attachment difficulties are exposed when enmeshment and codependency with parents exist. This leads to subsequent anger toward self and caregivers for remaining stuck in these patterns. Treatment for this group of young adults focuses on regaining the "age-appropriate position in their developmental trajectory" and developing "internal sources of self-esteem and identity, instead of relying on the borrowed ego strength of their parents" (Poa 2006, p.35).

A patient created an image in art therapy representing her relationship with her father. The title of the artwork, "We are not the same...so don't say that we are," seems to demonstrate the conflicts and challenges of separation-individuation. Figure 4.1 depicts the patient's face connected to the face of her father. During discussion of this image, the patient spoke about noticing qualities and deficits in herself similar to those she recognized in her father. She spoke about the difficulty of finding out who she was outside of her relationship with her father, and the struggle of becoming her own person.

Figure 4.1. Split face

Another patient created an image about her identity (see Figure 4.2). She summarized for the art therapy group what her image represented:

I don't know what my identity is. I have to discover it. That's why the white square is there. It symbolizes the infinite possibility of what I can become. The white square also represents the NA [Narcotics Anonymous] symbol, so I can become anything through my recovery. Outside of the square is dark because my past has been dark. My past has had lots of pain, lots of trauma, and lots of loss. It's part of who I am but it does not have to define me.

Figure 4.2. White square

Age of instability

Arnett (2004) contends that the high rate of residential changes points to the unstable nature of emerging adulthood. As young people move out of parents' homes to enter college or the workforce, their living situations change. Emerging adults seeking independence may do so by leaving their parents' home and seeking other living arrangements with friends or romantic partners. Young people who attend college may make several residential changes over the course of their education, including dormitories and college housing to apartments or houses near campus. The increase in cohabitation also contributes to residential changes during emerging adulthood. The transitional nature of emerging adulthood persists, yet a recent trend published by the Pew Research Center in 2017 indicates an increase in young adults living at home. This reflects how changes, such as delayed marriage and career instability, impact the economic circumstances of many emerging adults. This trend may also reflect changes in the economy and job market in recent years (Fry 2017; Vespa 2017).

Instability during this period may predicate high rates of anxiety and depression in emerging adulthood—frequent residential changes may lead to inadequate social support (Arnett *et al.* 2014). Many Compass patients suffer from severe personality disorders, usually oriented to Cluster B of the DSM-IV.[1] Although young, they already struggle with disabling symptoms of their disorder. There is often a history of multiple suicide attempts, self-harm, self-destructive behaviors, dysfunctional and unhealthy relationships, impulsivity, or instability that crosses into all areas of their lives. In addition to their core personality disorder, these patients also struggle with major affective disorders, anxiety, substance abuse, or eating disorders (Poa 2006). For these individuals, instability characterizes their internal experience and may be worsened by the unstable nature of external environments in the emerging adult stage.

Internal and external instability are depicted in a drawing created by an emerging adult (see Figure 4.3). She drew herself in a cage suspended by a thin chain, and it is unclear what the chain is connected to. She described the cage as a metaphor for depression. The monsters lurking below symbolize environmental stressors pertaining to relationships, school, and her future. The image is framed by darkness, reflecting feeling trapped in the cage and unsafe leaving it. She then changed the image to show herself climbing out of the cage toward a ladder leading upward, out of the darkness.

---

1   See www.mentalhelp.net/articles/dsm-5-the-ten-personality-disorders-cluster-b, for more information.

Figure 4.3. Suspended cage

Age of self-focus

Not to be confused with selfishness or self-centeredness, self-focus is a distinct characteristic of emerging adulthood (Arnett 2006). Young people are not obligated to family of origin duties, rules, and routines as children and adolescents are. Many do not yet have families of their own to be responsible for, or long-term employment commitments. This leaves time and space to focus on the self, and autonomy to take agency in managing their own lives. Self-focus also provides considerable freedom, as emerging adults do not have social obligations and responsibilities in the same way that adolescents and adults might.

Arnett (2006) notes that while emerging adults have new freedom from answering to others, self-focus should be in the interest of figuring out how to attain self-sufficiency that is essential to adulthood. Self-sufficiency prepares young people to be other-focused as they enter into marriage and parenthood. The freedom of self-focus is enjoyed with the knowledge of its impermanence, a necessary part of the process prior to committing to more enduring work and personal relationships.

Self-focus has mental health implications, as it creates the potential for low social support, which can lead to depression (Arnett *et al.* 2014). As young adults achieve increased stability in relationships, their perception of social support increases and depressive symptoms decrease inversely (Arnett *et al.* 2014; Pettit *et al.* 2011). However, young adults with deficits in obtaining and maintaining healthy interpersonal relationships may experience a sense of intense loneliness and disconnection. Many Compass patients have significant struggles in social and psychiatric functioning (Poa 2006). They often present with comorbidity consisting of multiple mood or thought disorders, substance use disorders, or personality disorders. Past failures in social functioning, transient relationships with treatment providers, or intense susceptibility to stress impede their ability to learn from past experiences (Poa 2006). For these individuals, repeated patterns of interpersonal dysfunction point to epistemic mistrust.

Tanner (2006) notes that the demographic shift of delayed relational commitments may lead to better partnership matches than earlier in life; however, delayed marriage and parenthood may also present risks for mental health due to the postponement of protective factors inherent in committed relationships. Additionally, self-focus may lead to difficulties prioritizing others over self and difficulties compromising, which is necessary for healthy partnerships.

For example, Sheila suffered from depression and identified intense feelings of isolation and loneliness. She lived alone in an apartment near her college campus, and struggled with substance addiction and disordered eating. Sheila was extremely intelligent and creative, but following the end of a serious romantic relationship, she stopped attending all classes. The few relationships she was able to maintain revolved around drug use. In the art therapy group, Sheila created an image of herself, standing before a mirror, with her eyes closed (see Figure 4.4). She graphically described her drawing for the group. The figure on the left depicted a sober self and the figure on the right represented her problems. She included a bruised eye from lack of sleep, physical assaults, and running into walls or falling while intoxicated; an inflamed nose from ingesting substances; and bile dripping from the mouth representing vomit from alcohol binges and also her eating disorder. Both eyes were closed because her sober self felt shame examining her using self and vice versa. When she was in the throes of a substance and alcohol binge, she did not have the vision, clarity, or desire to see or appreciate her sober self. For Sheila, the self-focused freedom of emerging adulthood seemed to further exacerbate her social and psychiatric difficulties.

Figure 4.4. Mirror image

Age of feeling in-between

The process of transitioning from adolescence to adulthood takes time. Attaining full adulthood status, or at least feeling like an adult, is usually a gradual process, leaving emerging adults feeling stuck in-between. No longer adolescents and not yet considering themselves as adults, emerging adults are in-between. Young adults do not consider transition events like completing education or getting married as indicators for adulthood. Rather, financial independence, and the ability to make independent decisions and accept self-responsibility are top criteria for adulthood (Arnett 2006).

According to Arnett and colleagues, "feeling in-between might elicit feelings of depression and anxiety in some emerging adults, especially those who believe they should feel more adult at their current age than they actually are" (2014, p.572). Feeling in-between may equate to feeling stuck or trapped for some young adults. Stuckness in recovery is common to Compass patients, who are caught in-between the "confluence of their developmental stage, psychiatric illness, and inadequate care" (Poa 2006, p.31).

A patient drew a portrait of himself and a dark mass with tentacles stretching toward him (see Figure 4.5). He further demonstrated feeling in-between by writing lyrics from the song "Wake Me Up" by Avicii, which referred to a desire to skip past the current confusing and overwhelming stage of life to a time in the future when he will be more mature. The patient discussed feeling stuck in this phase of his life, with his psychiatric disorder represented as the dark, threatening mass surrounding him. He described feeling suspended here, uncertain about the outcome. There seemed to be some hope that there is another side that he can reach, when his emotional pain subsides and he is able to gain some wisdom from his struggles.

Figure 4.5. Portrait with dark mass

Age of possibilities

Arnett describes emerging adulthood as a time of optimism, when young people generally have high hopes for the future. Most believe that it is possible to find gainful employment and to attain marriage or long-term relationships. He notes that people from lower socio-economic backgrounds are more hopeful and tend to believe in the possibility of a better life than their parents, even those whose current situation is not promising (Arnett 2000b, 2006; Arnett *et al.* 2014). Young people who experience difficult family of origin conditions have the opportunity to physically separate themselves. No longer at the mercy of their parents, they can make decisions about how to direct their lives and form healthy attachments.

High optimism in emerging adulthood could be viewed as a resource during a stressful stage of life; however, the changing economic climate may render that optimism misplaced for young adults who are confronted with the possibility of unemployment and low-paying jobs in adulthood. While most young adults are optimistic about the future, those who are not may pose increased risk for depression and anxiety (Arnett *et al.* 2014).

Emerging adulthood is considered the age of possibility because the range of choices abounds more than in any other stage of life. Young people have the possibility of change, as they do not yet have fixed obligations that may propel them in the trajectory of previous decisions. Rather, in emerging adulthood the roads are open and the pathways are clear. For some, possibilities may be endless. However, while various emerging adults have the freedom to break free from unhealthy patterns in family environments, simply leaving home or moving to a new location is not sufficient to make lasting change. Young people may be limited in their capacity for change, as family of origin influences are far-reaching and not bound simply by geography or location. Moreover, the presence of mental illness may further complicate or impede transitions occurring in emerging adulthood.

A patient painted an image (see Figure 4.6) of layers of color from white at the bottom turning to light blue, then purple, and added a black sky with yellow stars at the top to represent hope. This directive is further discussed in Chapter 8. During the writing exercise, the patient connected the idea of hope with possibilities for her future. She wrote:

> Hope is the wide open space of possibilities. It is not contained to this earth alone but will spread as far as you can see. Even when you seem to be lost in the darkness far above, there are still glimmers of hope all around you shining through the void as beacons reaching out to you, beckoning you to persist through the seemingly endless darkness with the promise of a better existence.

Figure 4.6. Wide open space

Access to mental health treatment

As early as the 1980s, following the deinstitutionalization of chronic patients in the United States, the rise of young adult patients exposed the lack of mental health services to address their unique needs (Bachrach 1984; Pepper, Kirshner and Ryglewicz 1981). Since that time, both inpatient and outpatient psychiatric facilities have developed to address the specific issues of this population; however, discontinuity in the transition from child to adult mental health services continues to pose a problem (Paul *et al.* 2015).

Young adults ages 18 to 25 are less likely to receive mental health services than any other population—only about one-third of this population who suffer from any mental illness are actually receiving services (Center for Behavioral Health Statistics and Quality 2015). This deficit may in part be related to the lack of continuity of care throughout the transition from adolescence to adulthood as young adults face difficulties finding and utilizing appropriate treatment (Paul *et al*. 2015; Poa 2006). The emerging adult stage is relatively new; as such, healthcare systems have yet to catch up (Arnett *et al*. 2014). Since young adults are no longer legal minors, academic and parental authorities cannot require them to receive mental health treatment.

Many mental illnesses begin in late adolescence (APA 2013), and issues may manifest or be recognized just before the transition to adult services is required (Paul *et al*. 2015). A systematic review of the transition from child and adolescent to adult mental health services identified a lack of transitional care models for emerging adults and a gap in policy and practice. Paul *et al*. encourage support for the development of programs addressing mental health issues and prioritization of mental healthcare for young adults (Paul *et al*. 2015). Deficits in psychiatric care for young adults is problematic, as this inherently vulnerable population may "find themselves underserved, misunderstood, and mistreated" in the face of psychiatric illness (Poa 2006, p.29).

While the Patient Protection and Affordable Care Act (2010) made efforts to expand mental healthcare access and substance use disorder treatment in the United States, limitations still exist in young people's ability to receive treatment (Gehr 2017; Monaghan 2013; Salonera and Benjamin 2014). Due to the private specialty psychiatric hospital model, Menninger patients typically do not benefit from public healthcare policy supporting mental health treatment or extended dependent coverage. The relatively high socioeconomic status of the Compass patients does not omit the financial burden that many young adults face as barriers to access. Additionally, chronicity, complexity, and stigma persist and impede entry to treatment. Regardless of socioeconomic status, the disconnection or gap between child and adult mental healthcare systems continues to inhibit quality and continuity of care.

Mental health issues

In emerging adulthood, overall wellbeing increases. Many young men and women experience a peak followed by subsidence of substance use, and a decrease in problem behaviors. However, this coincides with a paradoxical increase in psychopathology during emerging adulthood (Schulenberg and Zarrett 2006). This may be explained by the heterogeneity of this stage. For some, emerging adulthood provides a fresh start with new contexts, social roles, and opportunities. For others, a decrease in supports and structure is a disturbing shock to the system, and prompts the emergence of psychopathology. Those with inadequate resources and limited opportunities may find that the abrupt jolt into adult roles and responsibilities in fact reduces a sense of personal freedom. In such cases, maladaptive behaviors may arise as the ability to cope is compromised. In emerging adulthood,

> more individual and contextual change occurs...than in any other time in life. And mental health, broadly defined, is best thought of in terms of moving targets, especially during late adolescence and emerging adulthood. It is not a coincidence that these changes in mental health and psychopathology occur during this major life transition. (Schulenberg and Zarrett 2006, p.149)

Transitions generally test coping capacity, and emerging adulthood is no exception.

Several psychiatric disorders manifest during late adolescence and early adulthood, including a number of personality disorders, mood disorders, and thought disorders (APA 2013). Mental health disorders are prevalent in young adulthood (Arnett et al. 2014). Occurrences of depression in adolescence tend to resurface in emerging adulthood, leading to a high recurrence rate during this developmental period (Arnett et al. 2014; Sheets et al. 2014).

Sheets *et al.* (2014) examined personality pathology as a predictor of depressive disorders in emerging adults. The study suggests that interpersonal hypersensitivity, antisocial conduct in adolescence, and social anxiety are three pathology factors closely related to recurrence risk of major depression in emerging adulthood. Young adults with interpersonal hypersensitivity may experience relationship deficits due to challenges establishing connection. Hypersensitivity in relationships may be underpinned by fear of rejection, abandonment, and judgment. People who are sensitive to judgment and scrutinize interactions create a bind as their actions may lead to paradoxical outcomes; they are likely to cause more conflict as they try to manage interactions and navigate relationships. These factors also link to Cluster B personality disorders, which are characterized by interpersonal deficits (APA 2013; Sheets *et al.* 2014). Relational conflict and stress make young adults vulnerable to depression.

Another factor contributing to depression in young adulthood is antisocial conduct, which leads to negative reactions from others and social isolation. Failure to achieve social competence, failure in interactions, peer rejection, poor academic performance, and conflict in parent–child relationships in adolescence place emerging adults at high risk for depression recurrence. Lastly, social anxiety contributes to this risk. As emerging adults leave their family homes, more peer support is required. Feelings of inadequacy and insecurity may lead to avoidance for those with social anxiety, which makes it difficult to establish peer support. Isolation increases risk for depression.

The study by Sheets *et al.* (2014) concludes with a call for programs for emerging adults that incorporate skills and strategies to help them cope with social deficits, interpersonal rejection, and social avoidance. It is of note that all three pathology factors examined (interpersonal hypersensitivity, antisocial conduct in adolescence, and social anxiety) pertain to how young people navigate social and relational contexts. Severe problems in social functioning are characteristic of persistent dysfunction in young adulthood.

Resilience

Resilience refers to a person's ability to adapt in the face of adversity. In emerging adulthood, resilience links specifically to the achievement of developmental tasks. It pertains to competence in meeting behavioral expectations in the various domains of psychosocial functioning. In this stage, "academic achievement, peer relationships, and rule-governed conduct, which have been prominent throughout the school years, remain salient; at the same time, work and romantic relationships, which are key developmental tasks of adulthood, are emerging" (Masten, Obradovic and Burt 2006, p.175). When resilience is present in adolescence, it typically remains present in emerging adulthood. It can also develop during and after emerging adulthood. The emerging adult period presents an opportunity to promote and foster resilience (Masten *et al.* 2006).

It is necessary to acknowledge barriers to resilience, including psychiatric disorders that can severely impair the achievement of these developmental tasks. As previously discussed, the presence of a high p factor suggests deficits in resilience, which indicates problems with epistemic trust and salutogenesis (Bateman *et al.* 2018). Compass patients are at high risk for resilience deficits due to the insecure attachment styles that many have adopted, and the correlating mental health vulnerabilities that hinder access to (and the ability to make use of) social and societal opportunities that would otherwise provide scaffolding for the transition to adulthood. For emerging adults the task of taking initiative and agency in life may conflict with the need to seek help from others. In treatment, this conflict between autonomy and independence is also present and leads to difficulty engaging in the treatment process. Compass patients are encouraged to collaborate with the treatment team, though some have difficulty acknowledging struggles and seeking support (O'Malley 2018; Poa 2006). As our colleague Flynn O'Malley notes:

> the task of engagement in collaborative treatment is truly daunting. Those emerging adults who most often are urged by others to seek psychiatric treatment have frequently already had multiple courses

of treatment. Such patients have often developed maladaptive patterns of thinking and ways of coping with their problems that make it difficult for them to engage and collaborate in treatment. (O'Malley 2018, pp.177–178)

Attachment and individuation

Tanner (2006) proposes the idea of *recentering* as an underlying process of emerging adulthood. Recentering is a multi-stage process that is linked to separation-individuation and ego development. It implicates a major shift in how the young person interacts with the social world and is related to mental health. During this process, "other-regulated behavior (i.e., behavior regulated by parents, teachers, and society) is replaced with self-regulated behavior toward the goal of adult sufficiency, the ability to meet the demands of adulthood" (Tanner 2006, p.22). Using a developmental systems framework, Tanner (2006) integrates the emerging adulthood stage into lifespan theory by focusing on the relational aspects of development.

Early attachment influences cognitive and social development in emerging adulthood. As discussed in the previous chapter, attachment styles derive from primary caregivers and have a lasting impact in emerging adulthood. When primary caregivers are sensitive, available, and reliable, young people develop a sense of self that is worthy, and a view of others as available and trustworthy; however, when primary caregivers are unavailable, inconsistent, unreliable, and misattuned, young people develop a sense of self that is unworthy and a view of others as untrustworthy (Bowlby 1982). As such, attachment issues are precursors and contributors to mental health difficulties. Attachment styles are linked to mental health in emerging adulthood (Lapsley and Woodbury 2016). Secure attachment has been associated with adaptive social and psychological functioning (Kenny and Sirin 2006; Lapsley and Woodbury 2016). In 2014, Konrath and colleagues identified a rise in emerging adults with insecure attachment styles, including dismissive, fearful, and preoccupied. Given the link between attachment and mentalizing, this increase in insecure attachment also suggests mentalizing deficits during this period. While primary attachments influence how young adults navigate the social world, attachment is not fixed. New, corrective experiences can teach emerging adults to relate to others differently, just as mentalizing capacity can change and grow.

Lapsley and Woodbury (2016) discuss social cognitive development in emerging adulthood, and name attachment and separation-individuation as the processes necessary for success. Achievement of these developmental tasks fosters the establishment of a workable conception of self and others and supports the development of identity, intimacy, and autonomy. Internal working models of attachment determine how emerging adults may interpret ambiguous interpersonal situations. These models drive social perception and support cognitive-affective assessment and interpretation of social interactions. Emerging adults with insecure attachment styles may cope with stressful situations by distancing from others instead of seeking support in the case of dismissive attachment, or they may seek support excessively and ultimately alienate others and compound their sense of abandonment, in the case of anxious/preoccupied attachment styles. Emerging adults with fearful attachment may express emotional distress without the willingness or ability to seek support from others (Lapsley and Woodbury 2016).

Whether or not a young person comes from a home where attachment needs were met, the transitions inherent in emerging adulthood are demanding and may impact a person's ability to cope and adapt. Schulenberg and Zarrett (2006) outline two paths of mental health in emerging adulthood. In the first, young people from homes where their needs are unmet and mismatched with the capacities of their families of origin may continue to struggle in emerging adulthood, or may use the transition to create positive change and find appropriate ways to meet their needs in contexts outside of the home. Another example of how mental health issues may emerge is in young people who have a healthy family life and are well matched and attuned to in childhood and adolescence, but leave the home and struggle to find ways to get their needs met in new roles and new contexts. Both situations potentially lead to mental health issues. Furthermore, the increased freedom and experiential nature of the period may also bring about the development of problematic behaviors along the way to adulthood.

Social cognitive development

Cognitive development continues in emerging adulthood. The brain is still developing and normal neurobiological changes occur in this period (Schulenberg, Sameroff and Cicchetti 2004). Complex thinking is critical for emerging adults, as they face issues and decisions that are complex in nature, nuanced, and ambiguous. These issues impact social functioning, work, and worldviews as young people make decisions to explore and clarify identity in these areas (Arnett 2000a; Labouvie-Vief 2006). While emerging adulthood is important for the formation of mature thinking structures, it is also a vulnerable period where distortive and maladaptive modes of thinking may crystalize in the absence of critical social and cultural supports (Labouvie-Vief 2006).

While basic social cognition begins in early childhood, complex social cognitive skills and flexibility continue developing in adolescence and throughout emerging adulthood. King and Kitchener (2015) examined young adult cognitive development in terms of three cognitive processes: cognition, metacognition, and epistemic cognition. Overall cognitive complexity is linked to mental flexibility. It requires the ability to perceive the subtleties and nuances in an issue; consider these in order to arrive at sound judgment about the issue; and remain open to change initial perceptions about the issue when new information presents itself.

Many patients in the Compass Program lack this flexibility. They may adopt black-or-white, all-or-nothing styles of thinking; they may struggle with arriving at sound perceptions of self and others; and they may lack the ability to shift perceptions when new information presents. Where mentalizing is lacking in emerging adults, mature thinking structures fail to develop. Mentalizing-focused treatment addresses these pervasive issues.

A case for mentalizing

As previously discussed, cognitive development advances in emerging adulthood as mental flexibility, reflective capacity, and adaptation of thinking to new information continue to progress (King and Kitchener 2015). Considering that many of the young adults hospitalized at The Menninger Clinic present with attachment issues (Allen 2013; Poa 2006), complex cognitive skills and cognitive flexibility may fail to develop successfully. Patients in this phase of life may lack the ability to perceive and consider differing perspectives, form sound judgment, or remain open to change based on new information, especially when deficits in epistemic trust exist. The ability to think, process, and adapt is compromised in the face of complex issues in social, work, academic, and personal arenas.

Emerging adulthood is filled with exciting possibilities and inherent difficulties. As young people develop cognitively, they need to learn new information to navigate the socio-cultural roles they occupy. This time presents a challenge for young people with psychiatric issues, as it exposes vulnerabilities and increases risk for prolonged problems in functioning (Poa 2006; Schulenberg *et al.* 2004). For these individuals, social cognition is underdeveloped, development of complex cognitive skills is arrested, and the ability for adaptive growth is limited. If a young adult lacks epistemic trust, their ability to take in new, socially communicated information is hindered as others are viewed as unreliable sources of information. Given the nature and prevalence of attachment and separation-individuation issues that impede social cognitive development during emerging adulthood, MBT is an appropriate response. MBT can help emerging adults by re-opening epistemic trust, spurring the development of healthy attachment relationships, and ultimately providing a sense of an agentive self who is autonomous and responsible for choices.

Art therapy also seems to be a natural fit to support the promotion of mentalizing in emerging adulthood because it provides opportunities for safe exploration of self and others, which can aid in the reopening of epistemic trust. Art therapy offers a process by which emerging adults can make themselves seen and known and understood by others, thus gaining tools to form corrective secure attachments. Lastly, art therapy promotes the development of agency and autonomy. Art therapy is engaging. It is active and experiential, similar to emerging adulthood. The art therapy process can be viewed as a metaphor for constructing an adult life worth living as young people develop and grow.

This comparison arose during a discussion in an art therapy group.

Therapist: What was it like to be a part of this art therapy group?

Group member #1: I didn't think we were going to derive as much about ourselves from responding to someone else's art, but there's a lot of information there.

Group member #2: I think it's super-cool that I can make something that I thought was meaningless while making it. I thought I was just doing it to do it. But then it gains importance and significance as I discuss it with other people.

Group member #1: That's really how I felt about my life before I got here. Like everything I did didn't have any significance. I felt like I only had one choice to make so it wasn't a big deal if I made the wrong choice because I didn't have another choice anyway. But now that I'm looking at the reasons behind all the decisions I made, my experience of the world is so different. So art therapy is a metaphor for life. That's what springs to my mind when I hear you say that.

Therapist: Like making meaning of something that—

Group member #1: That felt meaningless. My life felt extremely meaningless before I came here. And when I think about leaving here I worry my life will be meaningless again. I feel very endowed with purpose when I'm here in treatment.

Group member #2: Yeah. Keep living. Keep arting. And then reflect.

Group member #1: Quote of the day!

Therapist: I hear your concern about life after treatment. I imagine it will be harder to leave the structure and support of treatment. I have also seen you work really hard to use the tools you've picked up here, although the hospital is a different setting.

Group member #1: Yes, I have learned a lot. But I think it's going to be hard for me to pick up the tools when I leave. It will be easy for me to go back to what I did before because I like what is easy and convenient.

Group member #2: It will take work to use the tools, but you have them. I feel like I'm still trying to learn what those tools are for me. It helps to know that you have figured that part out.

Group member #3: Was it fun?

Group member #1: My old patterns? Yes, but not in the long run. They caused a lot of harm. Oh, did you mean this group? Yes, it was fun. But it was difficult, just like treatment. Just like life.

CHAPTER 5

Mentalizing-based Art Therapy Group

In 2013, we transitioned the art therapy group for Compass young adult patients into the MBAT group. Patients are referred to the group by the art therapists or members of their treatment team, or they are self-referred based on their interest in creative therapies. Patients walk with the art therapists from the Compass unit to the main building, which houses the multipurpose room where the MBAT group is held. The open group meets for 90 minutes once weekly with a maximum of ten patients. Upon commencement of each session, the art therapists introduce the group and give information about MBAT. The group boundaries, structure, and process are reviewed at each session as new patients often join the group. This helps to focus all group members on the tasks at hand. Patients are given an art directive related to mentalizing. There is time for individual art making, which is often followed by a reflective writing exercise and verbal discussion of the artwork and art-making process. The group closes with a checkout where the patients discuss their experience of being in the group, followed by cleaning up the art space. Patients are then escorted back to the unit and the therapists debrief and provide handoff to staff. Artwork is stored in folders in a locked cabinet in the group room, though patients are able to request their artwork to share with others. Chapter 9 further discusses the life of the artwork following the group.

Development of the mentalizing-based art therapy group

We developed the MBAT group based on a *Mentalizing Education* group led by Jon Allen and Michael Groat on the adult units at The Menninger Clinic, called *Fostering Secure Attachments and Mindfulness of Mind*. This group followed an eight-week syllabus of discussion topics about mentalizing (Groat and Allen 2013). Mentalizing is taught and practiced as patients learn about attachment, empathy, and mindfulness. We attended the group with the intention of adapting the mentalizing approach to art therapy, and were pleasantly surprised by the prevalent use of imagery to generate discussion. Many of the mentalizing group activities can be found in *Mentalizing in Clinical Practice* (Allen *et al.* 2008). These exercises encourage group members to mentalize about self and other group members and then the group's mentalizing process is discussed. As art therapists, it was a natural extension for us to create art directives based on each topic on the syllabus. The result is an eight-week art therapy syllabus, detailed in Table 5.1.

Table 5.1. Mentalizing-based art therapy group directives

Topics covered in eight-week syllabus	Corresponding art therapy directive	Description of art directive
Relating to others	Relationship with other/ dialogue (Chapter 6)	Create an image representing an impactful relationship Write a dialogue between self and other
Relating to yourself	Relationship with self (Chapter 6)	Create an image representing relationship with self, considering attachment style
Understanding mindfulness of mind	Landscape of the mind (Chapter 7)	Draw a landscape representing the mind, including current thoughts and emotions
Experiences of disruption and repair in attachment relationships	Attachment relationships (Chapter 6) Disruption and repair in attachment relationships (Chapter 6)	Create an image representing insecure and/or secure attachment relationships Depict an experience of rupture and repair in an attachment relationship

Appreciating different perspectives	Draw a sculpture (Chapter 7)	Draw the same object and discuss the uniquely represented perspectives to the same subject
	Response art (Chapter 7)	Choose an artwork and create response art, reflecting feelings evoked
Imagining core problems for treatment	Stuck place (Chapter 8)	Identify a core issue or stuck place and draw it, then change the image to make it feel a little less stuck
	What's in the way? (Chapter 8)	Create artwork responding to the question: *What's in the way?*
Authoring your life	Life as a book (Chapter 8)	Consider life as a book, movie, or music album and design the cover
Maintaining hope	Maintaining hope (Chapter 8)	Create artwork about hope, giving it a shape, form, and color
		Write about hope

Group membership

As described in Chapter 3, the Compass Program at The Menninger Clinic treats young adults ages 18 to 30. Compass provides assistance for emerging adults struggling to manage the transition from adolescence to adulthood. Patients are admitted with a variety of treatment issues including mood disorders, anxiety, addiction, personality disorders, self-harm and suicidality, gender identity and sexual issues, and self-esteem issues (The Menninger Clinic 2014). Patients face challenges associated with developing identities and difficulties in interpersonal relationships. Patients enter the program for treatment, diagnostic formulation, and future recommendations. The estimated length of stay for patients on the Compass unit is six to eight weeks; following discharge from the hospital many patients are recommended for additional long-term treatment, such as community integration programs, intensive outpatient programs, or residential treatment programs.

In addition to the MBAT group, Compass patients attend a *Mentalizing education* group and participate in other mentalizing-based experiential groups on the unit. Patients also receive group and individual psychotherapy, and attend a number of skills and experiential groups and family therapy (The Menninger Clinic 2014). Although various modalities are provided to patients, including dialectical behavior therapy, acceptance and commitment therapy, and psychodynamic psychotherapy, mentalizing is the backbone of the Compass Program.

Location/Setting

The MBAT group sessions are held in a multipurpose room. Although this room lacks some of the features that might make for an ideal art therapy space, it is sufficiently conducive to creativity. The room has a somewhat clinical appearance as it is furnished with white tables, wooden chairs, white cabinets, and a sink. It is used for various purposes and as such, the tables, counters, and chairs are wiped clean between usage, and the room is kept pristine and sparse. A large window provides ample light and overlooks a lawn with trees and a metal sculpture, as well as part of the main parking lot. The room is equipped with a variety of art supplies, which are kept locked in cabinets lining two walls of the room. There are some limitations on materials provided to patients due to hospital safety regulations—a sharps cabinet houses scissors, brushes, knitting materials, clay tools, and other art tools that are potentially harmful. These sharps are checked out by patients and returned at the end of group session.

Opening the group

Each group begins with a welcome and introduction. New patients may join the group at any time, so members are at various stages of treatment. When newcomers are present, we take extra time to explain what the group is about, discussing both art therapy and mentalizing. When all the patients have previously attended, the opening discussion is shorter. The initial phase focuses on setting the intention of active mentalizing throughout the group, and inviting a safe atmosphere conducive to creativity and open discussion. Our hope is to help each patient show up authentically. We share this aim with them as we review the nature, structure, and intention of the art therapy space. For example, the art therapist might begin with:

> Welcome to art therapy. Here, we use art materials to explore and express our thoughts, emotions, and experiences. This is a mentalizing group and it is also a process group. As you have learned, mentalizing is about reflecting. The artwork is used as a vehicle to mentalize about ourselves, others, our relationships, things that are keeping us stuck, and things that keep us going. An important aspect of the group is that we try to make it a safe space for people to be able to express and explore. In order to encourage that kind of environment, we ask that you make a conscious effort to suspend judgment of your own artwork and your peers' artwork. We try not to use value statements like: "that's good, bad, ugly, beautiful, this is garbage, I suck at this, etc." We believe that the artwork and the art process have inherent value. Art experience or skill is not necessary. Art therapy is not about making masterpieces or beautiful works of art to be hung on the wall. In fact, much of the artwork created in this space is very personal. We invite you to use the materials to openly explore.
>
> This group lasts about 90 minutes, and each week we will discuss a different mentalizing theme. This may or may not overlap with what you are currently learning about in the mentalizing group. You will then have time to create art around that theme. The themes are developed to encourage mentalizing, but sometimes patients come in to group and they have something in mind that they want to create. Feel free to use as much or as little of the prompt as you would like. The overall purpose is that this time is used to help you reflect.
>
> After art making, you will be invited to engage in a group discussion. You will be asked to share in the discussion in order to process the images, to make yourself known and to know others in a different way. The primary focus of this group is to promote active mentalizing, emphasis on the "active." We don't want to be passive, but exploratory and curious with ourselves and with each other. In this group, you can share as much or as little as you feel comfortable sharing; however, part of the treatment process is challenging ourselves in order to grow. We encourage you to practice openness

and transparency with the group, and to ask questions to try to understand one another a little better.

At times, patients who have been members of the group for longer are invited to provide an introduction to their peers. This keeps older members engaged in the opening stage of the group, as some may have heard the introduction for several weeks. Therapists may also ask senior members to provide a rationale for some of the guidelines stated.

Working phase

Next, patients are provided with a therapeutic prompt or art directive (see Table 5.1) related to mentalizing, and time for individual art making followed by verbal processing of the images. While we occasionally limit art materials due to the nature of the directive, patients generally have access to a variety of art media. Materials are laid out on the table prior to the group, including oil pastels, watercolor materials, paper, canvas, acrylic paint, collage material, charcoal, chalk pastels, clay materials, markers, and colored pencils. Patients are also encouraged to use additional supplies from the cabinets when appropriate.

During the working phase, patients sit around a large rectangular white table with art materials strewn about. Music can be heard playing in the background. Some patients immediately engage and become deeply involved in the art-making process. Others take longer to begin. If a patient seems to be stuck with a blank page in front of them for an extended time, therapists demonstrate curiosity. When asked what is happening, a typical response is, "I'm thinking" or "I'm not sure what to make." At times it is appropriate to encourage the slow-starter to "make a mark, and then another, and then another," allowing for the art to organically unfold. At other times, more discussion is involved. The therapist may ask questions about what came to mind when they first heard the prompt.

Processing the image: Using the art metaphor as a vehicle to mentalize

When possible, the group moves to a smaller table for discussion. The transition to a smaller, more intimate space allows everyone to see the artwork at close proximity. It encourages interaction, eye contact, and ultimately, group cohesion (Leibman 1986). Patients are asked to bring only their artwork to the table, following a brief tidying of the workspace. The artwork is shared visually in various ways—sometimes, patients set the work on the table and walk around to see each piece; at other times, patients sit around the table and hold up their artwork; occasionally all the artwork is hung up on the whiteboard so it can be seen as a whole.

In addition to the mentalizing themes explored, processing the artwork verbally is vital. From a mentalizing stance, visual art metaphors are used to gain clarity around mental states. Metaphors presented in the artwork make it possible for group members to explore their peers' thoughts and emotions. They are also able to share their own mental states visually with the group. The art metaphor is used to explicitly mentalize. Because patients are made aware of the focus at the beginning of each group, the process of mentalizing is demystified as they are "in on it." Therapists play an active role during processing, and model how to discuss the artwork. At the same time, the onus rests not solely on the group therapists but equally on the patients to make use of the group to practice mentalizing. The following prompts are used to elicit mentalizing through the art metaphor:

- Describe what it would feel like to be in someone else's image or to be a specific element in the artwork.

- Write about thoughts and feelings and curiosities elicited from the image.

- Consider and describe what it is about the image that is making you feel _____.

- Write about your peers' images in the first person.

- Generate dialogue with forms, figures, and elements in the image (e.g., if the tree in the drawing could speak, what might it say? What might make it say that?).

The artwork is an externalized object. It is removed from the patient who created it, providing distance and safety. Metaphors create safety in a similar way. They are indirect expressions with multiple interpretations. Consequently, discussing metaphors may feel less challenging or intimidating than making personal statements. While some group members elect to stay with the art metaphor, others more readily relate their artwork to lived experiences, current difficulties, and emotions. When questions and statements are made about the artwork, patients can decide how to respond. For example, a group member might say, "It would be so lonely to be stuck in this cave." The art maker can then choose to respond by discussing the image in terms of the metaphor (e.g. "the cave *is* lonely") or offer a more direct statement about their subjective experience (e.g. "*I* have been feeling really lonely this week").

Another level of processing occurs as patients discuss the experience of mentalizing in the group. Patients are asked what it feels like to be a part of the group and to have their image examined and explored. Sometimes patients report feeling understood and more connected to their peers. Patients have also reported feeling vulnerable or exposed in an unexpected way. When this is not explicitly stated, it may be felt in the way patients shift focus by telling jokes, complimenting peers' images, or changing the discussion from salient issues to lighter or unrelated topics. As previously emphasized, when this occurs, therapists call attention to it, as it is necessary to halt nonmentalizing (Allen *et al.* 2008). As therapists, it is important to recognize our own nonmentalizing tendencies and inclinations to move on too quickly, and one way to do this is to acknowledge how difficult and uncomfortable it can feel to sit with heavy emotions.

When misunderstandings and incidents transpire (which can be expected in most groups of people), the mentalizing therapist benefits from group members with a firmer grasp on mentalizing and higher levels of functioning. These mentalizing members are allies, with more grounded and accurate perspectives of their peers and the group experience. They help create an environment that is warm and caring, where "members express concern, sympathy, and gratitude for what they learn and receive from one another" (Karterud and Bateman 2012, pp.104–105). We have found that when a group succeeds at creating a mentalizing atmosphere, not only is the group room "filled with deep affection and love" (p.105), but this warmth abounds in us as well.

Closing the group

Checking in with patients about how they experienced the group is imperative to the process of closing the group. This discussion usually precedes a final tidying of the art room. It gives patients an opportunity to name feelings, and calls attention to what is taking place in the moment. When members clarify their personal group experiences, it provides space for varying perceptions and emotions, and demonstrates a model for holding multiple perspectives in mind. Mentalizing the group itself happens throughout the group, but special emphasis is given to this task at closure. Therapists may ask questions like: *What was it like to be a part of this group today? What did you notice about the interactions you had with peers? Is there something we missed that you would like for us to know? Is there anything you would change about the group today?*

When asked about their experience, patients respond in various ways. The following example demonstrates how a patient, Mark, used group checkout to clarify a surprising and differing reaction.

Therapist: What was it like to be a part of this group today?

Group member #1: It was a nice topic. Interesting.

Group member #2: Helpful.

Group member #3: It was one of the prompts I enjoy more.

Therapist: Mark, you've been kind of quiet. And since this is your first group, I'm wondering what it was like for you?

Mark: I'm kind of creeped out, to be honest.

Therapist: Yeah? What makes you feel creeped out?

Group member #2: Probably because you used charcoal!

[*Group laughter*]

Mark: [*Laughing*] The charcoal is also part of the reason I'm creeped out. It gets everywhere.

Group member #1: Charcoal is on your face now.

[*Group laughter*]

Therapist: It keeps spreading. Try not to move. Freeze!

[*Group laughter*]

Mark: There's no way to win with charcoal. Anyway, I felt really consumed by this. And now looking at this, I'm shocked by what came up.

Therapist: What about it makes you feel shocked, Mark?

Mark: It's just that thinking back to when I was making it, I felt like this [*pointing to drawing*] and then I made this drawing. When I look at it, it feels like me but that throws me off, startles me. I don't know if anyone can relate to that?

Group member #3: Sometimes when I make art about something, it feels more real to me.

Mark: [*Nodding*]

Therapist: I see you nodding. Does that connect to your experience?

Mark: Mmmhmm. Also I think I'm creeped out because I'm looking at a scary drawing. I didn't plan to make it like this, but here it is.

Group member #1: That has happened to me too. But I don't think I was drawing something scary, though. And it didn't creep me out. I painted about something sad and then when I looked at it I felt sadder.

Therapist: Sometimes when I create something, there's a different relationship than when I talk about it. The visual depiction of that thing—that thought or that feeling—makes it tangible. This may not be the same for you, but is that sort of like what you're experiencing? That this thing is outside of you now that you've created—

Mark: [*Interrupting*] Exactly! And it's inside of me, too. Like I can see what's inside now because this drawing is a reflection of how I feel. It's strange because now I've put it out there. The process kind of got to me. I felt absorbed in this in a way I haven't really felt absorbed by anything in a while.

Debriefing

Following the group, the art therapists meet to discuss and debrief. The purpose of this meeting is to reflect on the group and to identify successes and areas for improvement. We examine our mentalizing at various times in the group, and provide feedback about which interventions were conducive to mentalizing and which were not. At times, we write or create art to reflect on the process. The following is an example of an art therapist writing to process one of the first MBAT groups facilitated:

The group left me feeling exhausted, drained. I noticed my heart rate increasing when I had to ask the tough questions. What is it in me that welcomes confrontation and then shrinks from it? The girls were open with their emotions. Aware. One noticed feeling like she drags others down. She felt hopeful about hearing personal things from others and thought she would be able to eventually be as open. We talked about relationships. Focused on feelings. The guys were uncomfortable, sad, upset. One said, "We shouldn't be talking about this." I felt confused. This is exactly what we should be talking about! The hard stuff, the stuff that is painful. He identified feelings, but could not sit with them. The other patient lacked focus, disliked the medium because it was hard to control. We made a comparison to uncontrollability of emotions. Pastels are like feelings. Another guy looked tearful and asked to leave group to go to the bathroom, presumably to cry. He was visibly upset and did not want to talk about it. He called his image cliché. It was not, to me. It was dark and brooding. He mourned over a past relationship and could not share it with us. He identified sadness and I asked him to mentalize what the other may have felt—to which he replied "sadness, disappointment." Silence. That's when the group felt at its heaviest. The heaviness is in the silences. The clock ticked and I noticed a shift in the group. The group acknowledged it. We were all drifting in uncharted waters.

This type of personal writing and reflecting by the art therapist reiterates the importance of creating space for therapists to mentalize ourselves, to identify our own thoughts and feelings, as it is not always possible or advisable to share every thought and emotion that comes up in the group. Transparency is valued but we have to maintain professionalism and disclose with intention. While there are structured and unstructured measures to assess mentalizing (Bateman and Fonagy 2016) and supervision groups with colleagues from different disciplines, our post-group debriefing among art therapists is highly valued. Personal writing and art making is a natural tool for creative therapists to self-reflect.

Handoff

As members of an interdisciplinary treatment team, we identify essential information from the art therapy group to communicate to other members. This is typically shared verbally during a team meeting. Information communicated during a treatment team meeting might include a description of the artwork along with the patient's verbal explanation of the image, particularly content that relates to treatment issues and their overall progress. Their engagement and participation is shared along with their mentalizing capacity. A particularly expressive or hard-to-describe work of art may be taken to a team meeting or diagnostic conference. This can assist other team members in mentalizing the patient's experience. The documentation process also offers an integrated mechanism for communicating with other team members, as each patient's group participation is described in a weekly progress note.

Additionally, we walk patients back to the unit after group, and provide nursing staff with a general handoff to inform them of any issues that arose in the session. Unless appropriate, we do not go into detail. The focus for nursing handoff is safety. For example, we notify nursing staff if a patient who typically self-harms when anxious demonstrates increasing anxiety or creates artwork indicative of distress. After one particular art therapy session, a patient returned to the unit and went immediately to her room and punched herself in the face. Though a handoff was provided to nursing staff, she had exhibited no glaring evidence of distress at any point during the group or in her artwork. The art therapist received a surprising call from the patient's primary nurse shortly after, questioning what had happened in the group. This incident is a reminder of the severity of the difficulties our patients face, how disconnected they may be from their emotions, and their challenges communicating needs and seeking support.

Unstructured groups

There are many benefits to unstructured art therapy groups. At times we open up the group to free art making. In those instances, we have found that the effectiveness of the group is not diminished. During an unstructured group, patients may be invited to use the time to create "anything you wish to express" or "whatever is on your mind." This invitation is sometimes met with blank stares and blank pages; at other times, patients freely and immediately begin creating.

One unstructured group was laden with emotional content and patients became tearful as they shared in discussion. At the end of the group, a patient asked, incredulously, "Why did you make us do that? This group is so heavy all the time!" It was useful to have working knowledge of this particular patient's difficulty tolerating emotional distress, which he demonstrated in other areas of treatment. Nevertheless, we were taken aback by the accusation that we *made* him create what he did, as this was an open art therapy session where a theme was not suggested. Neither of us forced his hand to make the marks he chose to make on his page. We validated the experience of the group being emotionally heavy, acknowledging the painful experiences shared by the members and represented in the artwork. We also expressed wonder and some marked confusion about how the patient felt forced, apologizing along the way about anything we may have said or done for the patient to think he *must* create a certain thing, after which a rather useful conversation ensued about perceived expectations and self-agency.

We have also conducted open art therapy groups with patients creating artwork that remains in pretend mode, lingering at the surface of any meaningful or emotionally connected content. Even in these cases, the artwork provides a representation of something happening in the patient's internal world and is thus a catalyst for mentalizing—when patients are not expecting it, seemingly banal artwork can provide a springboard from which we can jump into mentalizing waters.

An example of this took place when a patient drew a cartoon caterpillar and butterfly in an art therapy group about change. Thanks to the cohesiveness of the group at the time, members were able to empathically challenge the patient's pretend mode, calling attention to his lack of thoughtfulness or connection to his image. The following demonstrates milieu therapy and explicit mentalizing at work:

> **Kevin:** I drew this caterpillar that turned into a butterfly and I used the watercolor.
>
> **Group member #1:** I like the colors.
>
> **Group member #2:** I notice the large eyes. I wonder why their eyes are like that?

Kevin: Oh, I don't know, I just wanted to give him really big eyes.

[*Laughter*]

Group member #2: Why?

Kevin: I don't know.

Group member #3: Could that represent that change is hard?

Kevin: I guess.

Group member #4: Or is it representative of change itself?

Group member #5: Do you identify with the caterpillar?

Kevin: Hmmm, I don't know.

Group member #3: Does the butterfly have buck teeth?

Kevin: Yes. I don't know why.

[*Laughter*]

Group member #3: I'm very curious about this. They both seem very tired. And they look like they're just trying, trying to be SO happy. Their eyes are bloodshot and bulging, and their smiles look a little stressed or forced.

Group member #2: Yes! Like it's really hard for him.

Group member #3: Looks like he's trying to be *really* happy.

Group member #5: The caterpillar's eyes make me feel a little stressed.

Group member #1: The eyes look tired. Or bloodshot.

Kevin: It's like he's fucked up on—

Group member #3: Is it drugs? It seems like they're on drugs.

[*Laughter*]

Therapist: Did you have any intention going into this process? Before you started, did you have an idea?

Kevin: Not really.

Group member #1: Does the white space in the background mean anything? To me it could signify that they're kind of lost in life because there is a lot of blank space.

Kevin: No, no, no. Like this whole part? [*Pointing to the background*]

Group member #1: Yes, the background.

Kevin: Oh, I probably should've done something there.

[*Laughter*]

Group member #3: You chose to not add something and I wonder why.

Group member #1: To me, it seems like they're lost.

Group member #3: Yeah, they look very lost.

Group member #1: They don't know where they are. They don't know where they're going.

Group member #6: Do you relate to the image at all or was it just something you drew?

Kevin: [*Laughing*] I don't know. I guess since you guys came to the conclusion that he's fucked up, I relate to that.

Therapist: Those were your words, right, Kevin?

Kevin: Yes. This picture is just... I don't know.

Therapist: It seems like the group is working really hard to understand your image and offer their perspectives. Am I getting that right guys?

Group member #6: Yeah, everyone is asking a bunch of questions, saying what they see in the picture and you're giving really short answers, Kevin.

Kevin: I know.

Therapist: What is that like for you? What is that about for you guys?

Kevin: [*Shrugs*]

Group member #3: I think it's kind of fun.

[*Laughter*]

Group member #3: In art therapy it's usually really deep and emotional. And it doesn't feel like Kevin is feeling any deep emotions connected to this picture. It seems more comedic and I enjoy exploring his artwork, from a comedic perspective. But also if it's not funny, please let us know.

Kevin: I don't know. Wait! Did you say people get deep and emotional in this group?

Group member #3: Yeah! People cry in here, man.

[*Laughter*]

Therapist: I wonder, though, if this process is reflective of how hard it can be sometimes to get in-depth with emotions?

Kevin: Yeah, with art. I'm not really comfortable with it. This is my first group, I don't know.

Therapist: I appreciate that you were able to do it, even though it's not something you do regularly. I guess I'm curious about your relationship to your emotions in general—

Kevin: I think I can express emotions, sometimes. Maybe not in a group setting.

Therapist: And what about the group setting makes it hard?

Kevin: Uhm. I don't know. There are a lot of people. I have been vulnerable in groups here and it's hard and exhausting, I'm kind of tired of it.

After this, a few group members validated how exhausting therapy work can be. The more senior group members called attention to Kevin's affective disconnect from his image.

In this case, although the imagery could be considered somewhat superficial, it still served as a vehicle to examine Kevin's resistance to vulnerability in groups. He was not able to avoid exposure but was gently prodded by peers' inquiry, and acknowledged his real concerns about becoming emotional. His peers were able to validate the challenges of doing therapeutic work and opening up in groups.

Structured groups

Several benefits derive from structured art therapy groups. In addition to providing assistance in getting started, themes can work well when there are time constraints. Structure can facilitate group cohesion and help members relate to one another. Additionally, themes can have multiple interpretations and thus provide some flexibility in meeting various needs (Leibman 1986). In the Compass MBAT group, the structure of themes provides a common focus and aim.

The decision to have structured themes in the MBAT group resulted simply from a place of not knowing. We were uncertain about many things, including our role as art therapists at Menninger, and how that fit within the psychiatric rehabilitation model and within the organization. We lacked the assuredness of our mentalizing role models. Five years later we are still uncertain, but more comfortable leaning into *not knowing*, which is, ironically, the essence of mentalizing. The syllabus from which we developed the art directives felt like a compass, guiding us on our voyage into the complex mentalizing terrain. Some years later, we are still on this adventure, with a better sense of direction than when we started. We no longer need the compass to steer us at every turn, but we are glad to have it at hand.

In the following chapters, the art directives are grouped into three parts. The first pertains to mentalizing about relationships with self and others. The second includes art directives that focus on the mind and perspective taking. The final set of directives involves mentalizing about treatment and life after treatment, including core issues, agency, and hope. Each directive is described in terms of the rationale of the art prompt, its connection to mentalizing, and examples of artwork and group processing. While structured art directives are not necessary for a mentalizing art therapy group, we have found that the art themes provide rich material for mentalizing. Our hope is that the directives described in the following chapters can offer some guidance for other art therapists who are drawn to mentalizing. We hope that this provides direction for those at the outset of this journey.

CHAPTER 6

Mentalizing Self, Others, and Relationships

This collection of creative art prompts relates to the interpersonal and intrapersonal. The directives included in this chapter are *Relationship with other, Relating to self, Attachment relationships,* and *Rupture and repair.* We begin with a brief review of the role of attachment in emerging adulthood, mentalizing, and art therapy. We then explore how patients receive education on attachment styles in psychoeducation groups. Finally, we present the art directives and how they generate mentalizing.

Attachment in emerging adulthood

A primary task of emerging adulthood is navigating the "ongoing dialectic between separation and connectedness" (Lapsley and Edgerton 2002, p.484). The process of separation-individuation in emerging adulthood involves shifts in family relationships in order for young people to achieve *relational autonomy*, a term first used by Josselson (1988), which is the desirable outcome of the individuation process. Emerging adults are at risk for fused, enmeshed, codependent relationships on the one hand, and isolation, disconnection, and complete detachment on the other. The goal is achieving mutually validating relationships where independence and dependence coexist (Allen 2013; Lapsley and Edgerton 2002). This extends beyond family relationships, as young adults learn to form social and romantic connections. Developing healthy attachments is a critical task in this phase of life; they are protective and impact mental health.

Education on attachment

Upon admission, Menninger patients are administered a battery of assessments, including the Relationship Questionnaire (RQ) (Bartholomew and Horowitz 1991). The results of this measure are included in Figure 6.1. Out of the 997 Compass patients assessed since 2012, the majority (84%) have insecure attachment styles. It may not be surprising that young adults in a psychiatric hospital have difficulties with attachment relationships, but it does indicate a need for education. Patients learn about the impact of attachment difficulties on mental health and the impact of mental health on attachment relationships in different avenues of treatment including individual therapy, milieu therapy, and through Mentalizing, Social Skills and Role-Play, and Trauma psychoeducational groups. As such, many become familiar with attachment concepts prior to the MBAT group. The education groups explore difficulties in attachment faced during this developmental stage, and, more critically, normalize attachment issues for those who have experienced trauma, as many Compass patients have.

During these education groups, patients engage in a discussion about how family of origin experiences impact attachment development and learn about various attachment styles: secure, ambivalent, avoidant, and fearful. These attachment styles are understood in the context of how a person views self and others (Bartholomew and Horowitz 1991).

Secure attachments are characterized by a person's experience of being known, understood, and accepted in a relationship. A person with a *secure attachment* views self as worthy and others as generally available, reliable, and trustworthy. Self-regard is derived internally in secure attachment relationships. Secure attachments provide a basis for regulating emotions, and balancing the dialectic between separation and connectedness (Allen 2013; Bartholomew and Horowitz 1991; Bowlby 1978; Lapsley and Edgerton 2002). People with *ambivalent attachment* have a view of others as dependable, available, and reliable, but view self as unworthy. This attachment style may create extreme dependency on others, diminished autonomy within self, and reliance on others for self-esteem. Emerging adults with *avoidant attachment* styles may view self as worthy, but others as untrustworthy or unreliable. This cultivates a sense of extreme autonomy and self-reliance, to the exclusion of forming meaningful connections with other people. *Fearfully attached* individuals view self as unworthy/unlovable, and others as untrustworthy, unreliable, or unavailable. This creates limited autonomy and limited capacity for relating and connecting to others (Allen 2013; Bartholomew and Horowitz 1991).

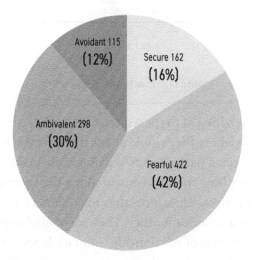

Figure 6.1. Compass attachment styles

The attachment styles explained to Compass patients are displayed in Table 6.1.

Table 6.1. Attachment styles

		View of Self	
		(+) Worthy, lovable	(−) Unworthy, unlovable
View of others	(+) Trustworthy, reliable, available, worthy	Secure attachment	Ambivalent attachment
	(−) Untrustworthy, unreliable, unavailable, unworthy	Avoidant attachment	Fearful attachment

An example of how these concepts are taught in education groups involves the therapist putting Figure 6.2 on the whiteboard, depicting various kinds of relationships along a spectrum. The therapist then discusses the lack of connection on the far right, the lack of autonomy on the far left, and the relationship in the center, where autonomy is balanced with connection. The group describes and discusses the various kinds of relationships in depth, paying attention to the cultural implications and biases inherent in our western view of what constitutes a "healthy" relationship.

Figure 6.2. Relationship spectrum

Patients are then invited to the whiteboard to place an "X" along the line, indicating where they would assess their current relationships. At this invitation, a patient or two will usually make a reasonable argument about how their placement along the spectrum depends on the relationship: with parents they may connect differently than with friends or a significant other. They are invited to put an "X" on the line for each kind of relationship. After each person has marked their place (or places) along the line, the group is invited to observe and reflect. Often, the line is heavily weighted with X's toward the far right and far left of the spectrum. A patient once remarked, "Of course our relationships are messed up. We're in a mental hospital!" This garnered laughter from group members while also opening up a discussion about what makes relationship issues seem inevitable where mental health issues are present, and vice versa. They acknowledge the perpetuating cycle: mental health issues make it difficult to form and maintain secure attachments, and insecure attachments contribute to mental health issues. Most patients seem to comprehend the gravity of attachments. It resonates as something that they can change, which many have not previously considered. They are motivated for exploration because they have experienced the impact of attachment and have an awareness of its implication for their lives.

Mentalizing-based art therapy and attachment

In preceding chapters, we discussed how mentalizing is linked to attachment theory. In the same way that primary caregivers model mentalizing, art therapists must also model mentalizing through image making and exploration. Havsteen-Franklin (2016) speaks directly to exploration of the image in art therapy. He writes, "the process of discovery through the image emulates something akin to good parenting" (2016, p.155). Mentalizing art therapists can influence mentalizing capacity and activate attachment through their thoughtful participation. The art therapist's attunement to the preverbal process of art making parallels the caregiver's attunement to the preverbal child's feeling states. In the art therapy group, contingent responding, marked mirroring, recognition of affective states, and expressed curiosity about the image engages group members in mentalizing processes that recreate optimal conditions for attachment (Havsteen-Franklin 2016; Springham and Huet 2018).

Art theme: Relationship with other

Directly asking young adults to create art about relationships invites visual reflection on attachments. In the *Relationship with other* group (see Table 6.2), we typically begin with a discussion about relationships and attachment styles (discussed earlier). The aim of the group is to explore attachment relationships and provide an opportunity for mentalizing both self and others in relational contexts. Patients are asked to think about significant and impactful relationships from the past or present, and then to choose a relationship that they would like to explore visually, perhaps one that feels challenging or unresolved.

Patients are invited to reflect on the relationship dynamics, considering feelings, thoughts, questions, conflicts, strengths, values, memories, and shared experiences. How do they interact or attach to the other person? How much or how little space does each individual have in the relationship? Do they feel known, understood, accepted? Does the other person? How has the relationship changed over time? Is there anything they would like to be different?

At times, materials are limited to looser, less precise media, such as chalk pastels or watercolors. At other times, patients are asked to represent self and others by using different art materials for each person. This promotes intentional thought about how the chosen medium relates to the person represented. Depending on the patients' needs, we may encourage abstract expression, challenging them to exclude human figures from their images and instead use lines, shapes, colors, and forms to represent the relationship.

Following the production of artwork, patients are provided with a writing reflection exercise (see Figure 6.3). They are asked to write a dialogue between the two people (self and other) as represented in the image, starting with, "If that person had a message for you, what might it be? How would you respond?" Patients can also begin the dialogue with a message they have for the other person. Patients are invited to consider what thoughts and emotions might drive the dialogue. This task encourages imagination and perspective taking. Essentially, patients must mentalize in order to complete this exercise. They can also engage in open/free writing without the structure of the prompt.

Table 6.2. Relationship with other

Description
- Think of a relationship from the past or present that is significant or has impacted you in some way.
- Consider the relationship dynamics. How much space did each person have in the relationship? How close or far would each person be? What emotions come to mind when you reflect on the relationship? How did each person interact with the other?
- Create an image representing the relationship.
- Complete a written dialogue between self and other (see Figure 6.3).

Processing/discussion questions

- How did you choose how to represent yourself and the other?
- What are your feelings when looking at the artwork? When reading the reflection?
- What was it like thinking about what the other person might say?
- What feelings do you think the other may be experiencing?
- Looking at your peers' work, what do you think it would be like to be the ____ in the image?

Message from other: _____

_____

_____

_____

Response (from self): _____

_____

_____

_____

Other: _____

_____

_____

_____

Self: _____

_____

_____

_____

Other: _____

_____

_____

_____

Self: _____

_____

_____

_____

Figure 6.3. Dialogue with the image

Adam's relationship with other

At 25 years old, Adam was admitted to the Compass Program following a serious suicide attempt. This came as a surprise to his family as he had not had intensive treatment or even outpatient therapy in the past. Adam was a polite, caring, intelligent young person, and quickly became a leader in the treatment milieu. This was not due to his possession of a commanding presence or because he desired to be followed, but he was well respected by peers and staff because of the respect and kindness he naturally offered to others. Adam, however, had a different assessment of his interpersonal experiences. He soon expressed difficulties relating to other people, noting that his relationships felt lacking in depth. Adam supposed that avoidance of emotions contributed to feeling unknown by others. He illustrated a relationship with other in an art therapy group (see Figure 6.4). The following is a reconstruction of the group discussion.

Therapist: Would you like to tell us about your image, Adam?

Adam: As I was making this, I noticed that I kept adding things to my drawing. Things I wasn't quite planning on. In essence, it's about trying to hold back the sea with a fence. It's just silly. It doesn't make any sense or mean anything. It's like my relationships.

Therapist: How do you mean?

Adam: Sometimes, the other person is the water and I'm the fence. In other circumstances, I'm the water and someone else is the fence. It just feels like there's always this passing through. There's nothing to hold on to, nothing fixed. And the sandcastle represents what the fence is supposed to protect, a mutually constructed relationship.

Group members were invited to observe the image and actively engage in discussion to clarify thoughts and perceptions. Open curiosity and identification of emotions elicited from the image were encouraged. The group was active as peers worked to understand Adam and share their observations of the image.

Figure 6.4. Adam's relationship with other

Group member #1: I feel sad when I look at it. Like something is slipping away.

Group member #2: I see a lot of movement in the drawing. The waves are moving, the clouds are moving. Also, it doesn't look like the waves have reached your castle yet. But it seems inevitable.

Group member #3: It's like impending doom, like we know what's coming. It makes me feel anxious. Powerless, if I were the fence. Futile.

Therapist: Adam, does any of that connect with your experience of the image?

Adam: The slipping away. I don't quite feel grounded in relationships. I don't know if I feel sad necessarily, but I do feel disconnected in some ways.

Here, Adam begins clarifying his emotions around relationships. He is able to take in different perspectives as the group offers their experiences of confusion elicited from the image and Adam's description of it. Adam is vague about which relationship he is discussing. To their credit, the group does not nod along passively, feigning understanding. Instead, they press for further clarification verbally, and maintain ostensive signaling of interest in the image.

Group member #3: Is someone supposed to be the fence and someone supposed to be the water? Who is supposed to be the castle?

Adam: I would interpret the castle as the relationship, something you build together.

Group member #2: Okay, so you're saying the castle is what you're building together and someone is the fence and someone is the water?

Adam: I'm not sure. I don't know. How do you look at it [*asking member #2*]?

Therapist: Let's pause for a second. Adam, I notice several questions being asked about the different elements in your picture. I think the group is trying to understand better how your image is connected to your experiences. Am I getting that right?

[*Group members nod*]

Adam: I think someone could be the fence, someone could be the water, and the castle could be the thing that's made together or maybe the relationship. I like the relationship as the castle, but maybe you're both the water and the fence.

Group member #3: I guess when I look at it I see the fence and the castle connected. Like the person has the castle as their secret and they are trying to protect it with the fence and the other person is the water. They're going to get to the castle and they're going to see your secret.

Adam: But if the water reached the castle it would just wash it away.

Group member #3: Exactly. So then there wouldn't be anything to hide. There's nothing wrong with the castle but it's made of sand on the beach. There's no real secret. The water will get to it anyway. So you're protecting something for no reason.

Adam: Hmm.

Adam seems to be co-constructing meaning from the image with the group. He remains open and thoughtful, considering interpretations his peers have offered while not immediately accepting his peers' feedback as his own perception. He seems to be in the process of authorship, finding meaning in the artwork he created. Next, the therapist brings it back to creator, Adam.

Therapist: Where would you be in the image?

Adam: At first I considered myself the fence.

Therapist: How would you describe the fence, Adam?

Adam: Immaterial. Sharp. Unfixed, since it's planted in sand.

Group member #1: It doesn't cover the whole thing because there are areas around it showing.

Adam: Yes. It's pointless.

Group member #3: It's only protecting one thing, so maybe other areas of the relationship are more open.

Adam: I think it really makes a difference if you're looking at the castle as something to hide or something to protect.

Group member #3: That's true. It could be something to protect.

Therapist: What was it to you? What was the intention?

Adam: To me, the sandcastle was the relationship you build with another person. It might just be made out of sand, but you've given it shape, so it's different from every other grain.

Therapist: I imagine it takes some effort to build a castle.

Adam: Yes, it's hard work to build a castle. And it's also an activity you see people doing on the beach when they're having fun.

Group member #2: What's the order that you made it in? What did you do first?

Adam: The fence, then the water, then the sky, the sand, and then the castle. The castle was the last part. Originally the plan was to make the fence and the water, and the rest I added along the way.

The metaphor of a sandcastle as a relationship is quite powerful. Adam speaks of building the relationship as both fun and hard work. It takes two people to build it, mutual effort. And yet, the castle is in the direct path of waves, its collapse imminent. Relationships come to an end. The fence is also likely to fall. It is built on shifting sand. The trepidation present in this metaphor seemed to echo Adam's anxieties about relationships.

As previously described, patients are invited to write a dialogue following the creation of the image. In this group, they were asked: *If you had a message for the other person represented in the image, what would you say? How might that person respond?* They were encouraged to continue the dialogue as long as they felt necessary.

Therapist: Were you able to complete the dialogue?

Adam: I didn't write a lot because I was thinking. So the only thing I wrote was what I would say: "I didn't know how else to be." And then I was thinking about it and wondering why I couldn't figure out what to say. I think it would say: "I couldn't figure out what to say and I didn't know how to say it." And the other person would say: "Any way you could say it would be all right. It's not a matter of how you compose it; it's what you're getting across." Something like that.

Group member #1: Would this be a friendship, a romantic relationship, family relationship? What were you thinking?

Adam: A friendship.

Group member #2: I think it's interesting you couldn't come up with what you wanted to write because you're so well spoken usually.

Adam: If I'm trying to say something that I think of as negative, I avoid saying it.

Therapist: What is it that you avoid?

Adam: Saying something that I perceive as negative, like sharing some aspect of me that I should ask for help with, but I won't. I'm working on this but it's difficult. And before I came here I could not and would not do it. So trying to think of a way to say that is still hard. Even though I know that the other person, someone specific in this situation, has shared a lot with me, even what they're struggling with. So I know that no matter how I say it, it doesn't matter. They would just want to hear what my struggles are and want to be there for me.

Group member #1: So there's some sort of barrier to saying it?

Adam: I just won't. It's strange to me. I'm not certain about what they would say, but I believe they would reciprocate in the same way that I have for them. They would support me.

Therapist: And what about that feels like something you'd want to avoid?

Adam: Then I think I would have to fully look at myself and acknowledge my problems as something more than what I can handle on my own

Therapist: What would that be like?

Adam: Scary. I know my problems are real but it's like connected threads. I can't acknowledge one thread without getting the whole tapestry.

Group member #3: Ugh. I know what you mean. All my issues are intertwined and connected.

Therapist: Adam, what does it feel like when you get the whole tapestry?

Adam: Overwhelming. Like holding back an ocean with a chain-link fence.

Group member #1: So the problems you're acknowledging are more powerful than the fence?

Adam: Well, the fence on its own is useless. You could go around the entire perimeter of the fence and it still wouldn't matter. It's a chain-link fence, so water would go straight through. It doesn't hold anything.

Group member #3: It's true. It's pretty futile that it's there. Like, why would it even be there?

Adam: Yeah. It's pretty stupid.

Group member #2: You said you would be the fence in the image and also it has been described here as futile. Do you feel that way?

Adam: [*Laughing*] I think you know the answer to that question. But yeah, I feel like the fence. I feel like some part of the sandcastle too because it's a communal construction.

Therapist: The image seems complex. The more we discuss it the more curious I become and I'm noticing a lot of questions from the group, too. Really, it's still a bit difficult for me to understand how it connects to you and your experiences in relationships. I find myself having more and more questions.

Group member #2: I agree. I feel confused.

Adam: Well, I'm not in treatment for any one specific reason. I'm here for a network of things that were manageable on their own but all together and without dealing with them, my issues just feed into each other to create this nasty little space for myself.

Group member #3: I see. All my issues are intertwined. But I think you allude to things a lot too. It makes it hard to follow sometimes. Like, you'll use a metaphor to explain, but it's hard for me to know from the metaphor what you might be thinking. So then I just apply my own interpretation to it.

Group member #2: [*Nodding*] And when you speak vaguely, it's hard to understand.

Therapist: That's a good point. It can be easy to make assumptions. We can naturally apply our own experiences and explanations. There seemed to be some of that happening now, but I also noticed you guys were really trying to understand. Adam, what's that like for you to hear this feedback from the group?

Adam: I know I can be vague and I try not to be.

Therapist: When you are being vague, what do you think that's about for you?

Adam: I'm not really sure, but I think sometimes I do it to avoid.

Adam's image elicited curiosity from the group. He described the process of forming the image and writing the dialogue. His rich visual metaphors prompted reflectiveness and some confusion as Adam and the group worked to understand them. The emergence of several of Adam's core treatment issues is present in this discussion, such as the difficulty making his emotions and challenges known to others, even close friends, which contributes to feeling disconnected and isolated. The level of openness in the group at the time made it possible for peers to engage honestly and share their confusion about the patient's roundabout manner of speaking. To his credit, Adam was able to admit that part of his vagueness was about avoidance, a theme that surfaced in multiple areas of treatment. This theme also emerged for Adam in a later art therapy group, where he spoke further about this issue, and which we continue discussing in the next section.

Tanya's relationship with her sister

In Adam's case, his lack of disclosure about a specific relationship was underpinned by challenges he faced being truly seen and known by others. In many cases, however, patients are able to depict important relationships that they wish to examine and reflect upon. Another patient, Tanya, used this exercise to explore her relationship with her sister (see Figure 6.5). She represented herself as a small clay ball, placed under a piece of tape. The ball was described as plain, simple, and unnoticeable. Her sister was represented as a similar-sized clay ball, except Tanya took the time to stick multicolor feathers into the malleable ball of clay. She described the feathered ball, and her sister, as vibrant, explosive, attractive, and the focus of attention. Tanya used this imagery to speak to her sense of invisibility in her family. When asked to express her affective response to the sculptures, she identified feelings of anxiety, anger, and resentment. In this case, Tanya's sister had achieved the developmental milestones of emerging adulthood. She was living a healthy and seemingly perfect life, according to Tanya. In discussing her artwork, she began to explore feelings of jealousy and inadequacy and perceived criticism from her family.

Figure 6.5. Tanya's relationship with her sister

Art theme: Relating to self

The next art directive encourages reflection on relating to self (see Table 6.3). Patients are asked to consider their self-relationship in terms of attachment. We explain that attachment relationships are not solely about how people connect to others, but also about how they connect to themselves. A person may have a secure or insecure attachment relationship with self. How individuals relate to self is the basis for autonomy and self-reliance (Groat and Allen 2013). Emerging adults with secure internal bases have self-empathy and self-awareness, are attuned to their emotions and needs, and are able to self-soothe and offer comfort, encouragement, compassion, and acceptance toward self. Emerging adults with insecure internal bases may avoid or dismiss their emotions, lack self-awareness, employ self-criticism, engage in self-neglect, or even act abusively and in harmful ways toward themselves.

During the initial group discussion, patients are asked to consider how well they know, understand, and accept themselves. Are they able to be honest about emotions, thoughts, needs, and desires? How do they treat themselves? What might their actions toward self communicate? Are they critical? Harsh? Compassionate? Forgiving? Do they have a strong sense of identity? Group members are invited to create artwork reflecting their self-relationship. The goal of this directive is to create a space for patients to engage in mentalizing about the self.

Table 6.3. Relating to self

Description
• Think about your relationship with yourself. Are you self-aware, critical, accepting, kind with yourself? Do you know yourself very well? How do you treat yourself? How much do you understand about yourself?
• Create art to reflect your relationship with yourself. You can think symbolically/abstractly.
Processing/discussion questions
• How did you choose how to represent your self-relationship?
• What are your feelings when looking at the artwork?
• Looking at your peers' work, what do you think it might say about their self-relationships?

Adam's relationship with self

Figure 6.6 depicts Adam's image of his relationship with self. He explained that all three figures represent parts of him. The figure at the very left of the page is the self that others know and see him as, standing upright, moving forward. The other two figures are less well known to Adam and to others. During the MBAT group, he explained his drawing.

> **Adam:** What I was trying to convey is that I'm avoiding myself, in a way. It represents entanglement with issues that have become my identity. Sometimes I feel like so much of what I do that is negative, my fixation on the negative, has become me, in a way. It makes me feel trapped, like I sort of become the issues.
>
> **Therapist:** Trapped in what way?
>
> **Adam:** I feel trapped in my patterns and my history. There are things that I almost conjure up, they exist to me but they don't really exist. That would be the shadow figure.
>
> **Group member #1:** Which one is you?

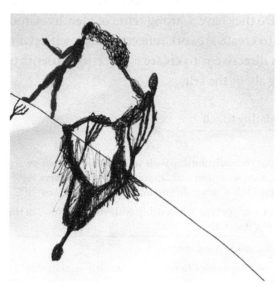

Figure 6.6. Adam's relationship with self

Adam: I'm all of them. This is all me. The creepy little demon guy in the center is what I've associated myself with in the past.

Group member #2: You're the demon, too?

Adam: Not really a demon, just kind of a shadowy self that's not quite there but still actively engaged in holding back my actual identity. And then the idealized self in front is what everybody wants me to become, but what is that? What is the ideal self? What is that to you? To me? What is my idea of my ideal self? Well I don't know! Does it even matter to me at all? I have issues and flaws that I try to avoid recognizing or dealing with, but they're still a part of me. And the shadow is reaching out and hiding all of the issues. Even when you get to where you want to be, there's always going to be something else to ensnare you. That's the thing just underfoot in the front, waiting to trap me. I try to avoid it, pretend it's not there, but it is.

Therapist: I notice you've spoken about avoidance a few times in this group and in other groups too.

Adam: This makes me think of avoidance. I'm avoiding myself. Making this got me thinking about how I speak in a way that is vague. It is an avoidant way of speaking. I'm not actually talking about anything real. I got into a huge habit of always doing the avoidant tactics of speaking, of getting people to meander and talk about themselves. Anything, anything at all to just not talk about me. And even to the extent that you start doing that enough times and you avoid even the good emotional states. You avoid happiness, sadness, so many things. Both the negative and the positive become things to avoid.

Therapist: What is it about speaking more directly that makes you want to avoid it? What's the function of that avoidance for you?

Adam: The function of it is to maintain the familiarity.

Group member #1: Of not being known? Familiarity of—?

Adam: Maybe of not being known, but also the familiarity of the person you know that other people know you as and need you to be.

Group member #3: What other people? Family? Friends?

Adam: Everyone! Most of the people in my life see me as this [*pointing to the figure in front*]. They don't know about all this other stuff [*pointing to the rest of the image*].

Group member #1: So is the thinking, "the more vague I am the less chance I have of ruining their perception of me?"

Adam: Yeah, it's just that you get accustomed to behaving in a certain way around people. But the avoidance in my picture is just so familiar, so it's easy to go on doing what I've always done, even if it's destructive. And that sort of avoidance, that destruction, it does prevent me from experiencing a lot.

To make this image, Adam engaged in mentalizing by thinking about his relationship to different aspects of himself, including what he shows to others and what he keeps hidden. He identified an idealized self, representing who he perceives others want him to become; he notes that he is unsure what his ideal self would be from his own perspective. By creating the image, he comes into contact with his history and patterns, which were otherwise uncomfortable for him to examine. Through the discussion process, Adam begins to identify his relationship with avoidance and its impact on relating to self.

Art themes: Attachment relationships and rupture and repair

The following art prompts invite patients to depict various attachment relationships and experiences of rupture and repair within them. For the first prompt, patients are invited to depict a secure or insecure attachment (see Table 6.4). A modification of this directive is to ask patients to create two images representing both secure and insecure attachments. This variation can be processed and discussed by grouping the secure attachment images together and the insecure attachment images together. The group is encouraged to look for themes in the artwork and to focus on the feelings elicited by the images. The second directive (see Table 6.5) asks patients to depict what rupture and/or repair look like in a relationship. They are invited to consider experiences of conflict and resolution in past or current interactions.

Table 6.4. Attachment relationships

Description
• Discuss secure and insecure attachment. How do you feel in each kind of relationship? Consider attachments with parents, friends, significant others, etc.
• Create an image of an attachment relationship. Optional: Write a response to the artwork, focusing on thoughts and feelings elicited from the image(s), or write about what it feels like to be in each type of relationship.
• Modification: Create two images to represent secure and insecure attachment styles. Group together secure attachment artwork and insecure attachment artwork to discuss themes and feelings elicited.
Processing/discussion questions
• How did you choose which relationship to depict?
• What emotions arise when looking at the artwork?
• Are there similarities or differences in the depictions of secure vs. insecure relationships? Do you notice any themes or consistencies?

Table 6.5. Rupture and repair

Description
• Group members are invited to use art materials to represent an instance of rupture and/or repair in an attachment relationship.
Processing/discussion questions
• How did you choose which relationship to depict?
• How did you decide to focus on rupture, repair, or both?
• What feelings are evoked when looking at the artwork?
• Looking at your peers' work, can you relate to their experiences of rupture and/or repair?

June's relationship with her boyfriend

A patient, June, explored her relationship with her boyfriend (see Figure 6.7). In individual therapy, June began discussing a pattern of tumultuous relationships. Prior to hospitalization, she had moved away from her hometown and family to be with her boyfriend. A series of decisions led to eventual homelessness. June and her boyfriend lived in her car and both struggled with addiction. After June reconnected with her parents, they convinced her to go to treatment. She reluctantly agreed.

June continued exploring relationship patterns in the MBAT group. In response to the attachment relationship art prompt, she created an image about her relationship with her boyfriend. June represented herself as a pink line originating from the upper left corner of the page and her boyfriend as a blue line originating from the bottom right corner of the page. The two lines twist and the colors blend together to form a purple center, which she stated represented their relationship. June described this image as a symbol of the love they felt for each other. The group was curious about the center of the image. When therapists encouraged the patients to describe it, they used words like: wrapped up, coiled together, and fused. June agreed that it becomes more difficult to distinguish one line from the other as it spirals into the center. A group member offered that the center of the drawing reminded him of the eye of a storm. June connected with this and responded that it was not always stormy but over time it had become dangerous for them to stay together. June stated that this relationship meant everything to her, and the end of the relationship was devastating. She explained that she loved her boyfriend so much that she had given up her job, friends, and family to move to a new place to be with him. She reflected that she becomes lost in the intensity of relationships, and spoke about her voracious desire for acceptance and love. Initially June described this as a secure attachment; however, the group discussion about the artwork gently revealed relational patterns that June was able to recognize as unhealthy. She tolerated her peers' reflections because they were focused on the image. She was curious about her peers' reactions to her artwork, and willing to mentalize about relationship patterns through exploration of the image. The art offered a way for her to look at various aspects of her relationship from the inside out and the outside in.

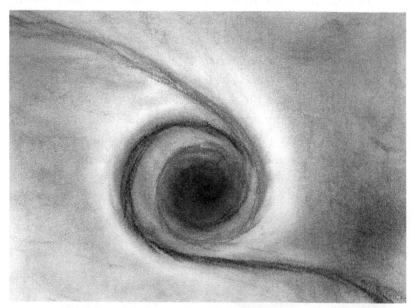

Figure 6.7. June's relationship with her boyfriend

Ruth's ruptured relationships

An example of the *Rupture and repair* group directive is illustrated in Figures 6.8 and 6.9. In these images, Ruth explored conflict in friendships that preceded her suicide attempt and subsequent hospitalization. She was desperate for connection and her attempts at pulling people closer often pushed them further away. Despite longing for acceptance, she related dismissively and experienced extreme difficulty trusting others. She reported that she can be impulsive and often has difficulty controlling intense anger, usually underpinned by fear of rejection or abandonment. Ruth recognized her reluctance to make use of therapeutic spaces, like group and individual therapy, to explore and help sort out her difficulties in relationships. She was active in the art therapy group and noted that she finds the production aspect of art therapy helpful; making something to represent herself and then talking about it helps her to be more reflective.

In the MBAT group, Ruth made two paintings about disruption in a friendship. In the first (Figure 6.8), she identified feeling disconnected from others and feeling pain around attachment, which contributes to her reluctance to explore relationships. The image shows Ruth looking at herself and the other person in the relationship from a distance. She recognized the disconnect between the two figures but also the positive feelings. She noted feeling like an outsider looking in and also recognized the value of reflection, though it was difficult for her to do. In the second painting, she drew herself and an amorphous central figure, representing a former friend (Figure 6.9).

Figure 6.8. Ruth's first drawing of disrupted friendships

Figure 6.9. Ruth's second drawing of disrupted friendships

The following is the therapist's recollection of the group discussion.

Ruth: This is my piece. I started two or three different times before I did this. I was trying to draw a person but I realized I can only remember certain parts of their features because thinking about their entire face together makes me really anxious, so I can't think of what they look like entirely, so I decided to paint this blob in the center. And myself in the corner.

Group member #1: So is this a person from your life?

Ruth: It's an ex-best friend. But he's not the problem; I'm the problem. That's me in the corner, freaking out. There's a lot of confusion, which is why it's kind of blurry and messy. I can't blame my issues on anyone else. It's how I handle things that causes problems.

Therapist: What do you guys make of the central figure, the amorphous dark shape in the center?

Group member #2: It's terrifying. That looks scary.

Therapist: Can you say what feels terrifying about it?

Group member #2: Looks like Ruth is being attacked.

Ruth: Well, it is terrifying. The fact that I couldn't even draw their face is because I'm scared of facing them. I think it actually might be the other way around, that I'm attacking them too.

Group member #3: I see it like you're the one attacked, because of the size of you. It also reminds me of your other drawing from before, where you were being attacked by several people.

Therapist: What do you make of your peers' response that you are the one being attacked?

Ruth: I don't know. It makes sense because I'm smaller, but it feels like I'm the one who has screwed up the relationship beyond repair. My actions have caused hurt. But also I can't tell what is real and what is just in my brain. It's easy for me to demonize people and also easy for me to idolize people, so I wrote "happy?" because I don't know if I actually was happy in this relationship.

Group member #4: For me, it's easy to distort things in my mind. That makes it so confusing.

Ruth: It's really dark because I don't know what to do. I can't fix anything.

Therapist: You can't fix anything. Can you say more about that?

Ruth: I'm sorry, that's an absolute. Well, it feels like I can't fix anything with this person while I am in treatment, because they don't want to talk to me, because it's painful for them. But I feel I need to fix things. Now. So I'm really stuck.

Therapist: What might that feel like? Not being able to fix things but feeling an urgency to? Not being able to communicate with the person because they feel hurt? Being uncertain about how things might turn out?

Group member #1: Frustrating.

Group member #2: Anxiety. Like, intense anxiety.

Group member #4: I might feel shame or guilt if I know I did something wrong.

Group member #3: The body of the central figure stands out to me. It looks like it can change, this shape-shifting creature that is unpredictable.

Ruth: The relationship is unpredictable to me. I don't know what's going to happen, and that's the hard part, not knowing. I do feel anxious and ashamed and confused.

Group member #2: Your mouth is open in the picture. Would you be saying anything?

Ruth: I don't know, maybe screaming. I yell at people. I'm so angry at them.

Group member #3: It looks like these lines could be sound waves coming from the little person in the corner. Like she's raging.

Ruth: Probably.

Therapist: And what makes you feel angry?

Ruth: They're gone. They seem to always leave me. I know that I have a part in it, but it keeps happening. That makes me angry with myself, too.

Lanie's rupture and self-repair

Another patient, Lanie, completed an image of repair in regards to herself (Figure 6.10). She made a fairly concrete depiction of the process of emotional healing during the treatment process. Lanie drew a broken heart with a needle and thread stitching it back together. She spoke about feeling relief that she was on the mend. She reported feeling proud that she was making progress in treatment for the first time. She also noted that the process was painful but necessary. When a peer asked who would be holding the needle to do the stitching, she replied, "I am. It has to be me doing the work. Before, I relied on other people to solve problems for me. I'm starting to feel more capable to do it for myself."

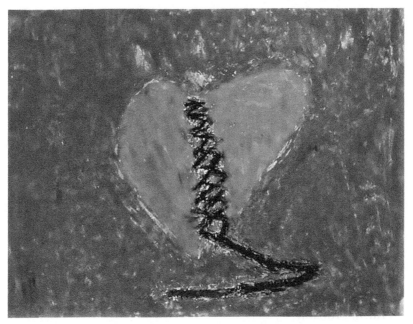

Figure 6.10. Lanie's rupture and self-repair

CHAPTER 7

Mentalizing the Mind

This collection of art directives encourages the mentalizing practice of *holding mind in mind* (Allen *et al.* 2008) or reflecting on the mind of self and mind of another. We explore mindfulness, its relevance in the Compass Program, and its connection to mentalizing. The art prompts detailed promote mindful attention and perspective taking.

Understanding mindfulness of mind

The concept of mindfulness is common in current psychology and loosely defined as conscious awareness of and intentional attention to the present moment. It involves a nonjudgmental noticing of present experiences and events, as well as flexibility about the source of attention and focus. With origins in Buddhism, mindfulness is a broad concept that relates to the here-and-now (Brown, Ryan and Creswell 2007). The practice and understanding of mindfulness is foundational to various therapeutic approaches such as dialectical behavior therapy (Linehan 1993), acceptance and commitment therapy (Hayes, Follete and Linehan 2004), and mindful self-compassion (Neff and Germer 2018). At The Menninger Clinic an outdoor labyrinth has been created specifically to encourage mindfulness. Meditation groups and yoga classes, which are also rooted in mindfulness, are offered throughout the week. Similar to mentalizing, mindfulness is woven throughout treatment on the Compass unit.

Though mentalizing involves mindfulness, it differs because mentalizing is solely focused on mental states. Mentalizing requires paying mindful attention to thoughts and emotions; reflecting on and understanding drives and motivators; and maintaining a curious, nonjudgmental, open-minded attitude of compassion for self and others (Allen *et al.* 2008; Groat and Allen 2013). Diverging from mindfulness, mentalizing is not exclusive to the present moment; we can mentalize about the past, present, and future. It is mindfulness about mental states, concentrated on the minds of self and others (Allen *et al.* 2008). Mentalizing is considered *mindfulness of mind*, described as mindful awareness and attention to thoughts and feelings in self and others (Allen *et al.* 2008).

Mindfulness is also not new to art therapy. The application of mindfulness to art therapy spans the length of several decades and has been applied to various populations (Rappaport 2013). Expressive therapies generally cultivate intentional awareness to the present moment, for both patient and therapist. Therapists can mindfully attune when they engage in practices such as reflective writing or reflective art making. Arts therapists who include mindful meditation in their work often have a deep commitment to this practice. Franklin (2010) writes of being mindfully attuned and present with the artwork and to the verbal, visual, and nonverbal communication of the patient. He uses mindful, empathic art making to attune to patients and reflect back difficult emotions. Many others precede and follow in that tradition (see, for example, Fish 2008; Lachman-Chapin 2001; Moon 1999).

In MBAT, explicit mindfulness is the function of the art therapist, who openly demonstrates this with patients. The art therapist shows patients "how to be mindful of their own actions and thoughts about what is being revealed in the image" (Havsteen-Franklin 2016, p.150). This is accomplished by paying attention to the artwork; expressly asking about and sharing present-moment thoughts and emotions; and reflecting on reasons for these thoughts and feelings with acceptance and persistent curiosity.

Art theme: Landscape of the mind

A key function of the MBAT group is using the art process and product to clarify mental states. This process is illustrated by one of the mentalizing themes addressed in the group *Landscape of the mind* (see Table 7.1). The art therapists facilitate discussion on the idea of *holding mind in mind* (Allen *et al.* 2008). The group is invited to think of thoughts, feelings, obstacles, and strengths, and to represent these elements in a landscape.

The metaphor of the mind as a landscape provides ample material for mentalizing. Group members are encouraged to consider the concept of landscape and given the creative freedom to move from topography to other mind representations. Patients have created seascapes, mountainous terrain, deserts, islands, urban sprawl, cityscapes, mazes, and even a circus. The *Landscape of the mind* group includes a writing component. Each patient is asked to write about their landscape, considering feelings and thoughts elicited from the image. Patients respond by considering what it would be like to exist inside of each image. They also write any questions or curiosities inspired by the image. Patients then rotate seats and view everyone else's images, one at a time. They write a response about each piece, including anything they may be curious or confused about, and imagine what it would be like for them to inhabit their peers' images. They then fold the page over after writing, to prevent others from reading or being influenced by what was previously written. After each patient writes about each image, the artist is asked to review what the group wrote and to share their reactions. Patients have the opportunity to clarify and share about their process and intentions.

Creating a metaphor requires imagination and creative thinking. The process demonstrates mental flexibility, as patients make connections between their internal experiences and relatable experiences in the external world. Metaphors provide safety for patients to discuss difficult experiences and emotions by offering distance and freedom to explore authentically. Art metaphors also encourage discussion about things that might get missed in verbal discussion. In the MBAT group, the metaphor itself is discussed as well as all the elements in the image used to create the metaphor (e.g., size, color, spatial relationships, omissions, inclusions). This allows for deeper understanding of the metaphor and its creator. Discussion of patient experiences in the group promotes further processing and consideration of multiple perspectives.

Table 7.1. Landscape of the mind

Description
• Consider what your mind would look like as a landscape. How would you represent your current mental state, thoughts, and feelings?
• Create art to reflect this landscape. It could be a place you know or an abstract representation. Think about what kind of terrain would represent your mind (e.g., peaceful countryside, turbulent ocean, circus, desert, urban sprawl, etc.).
• Written reflection: On notecards or sheets of paper, write down what it would feel like to be in your landscape. Then swap seats and write about what it would be like in other group members' images. Write down thoughts, feelings elicited, and questions about each image.
• Read reflections from your peers and share your perceptions and offer clarifications where necessary.
Processing/discussion questions
• What are your reactions to your peers' feedback? Is there anything you'd like to clarify? Anything that you connect with?
• Which emotions capture your experience?
• What was it like to write about your peers' images?
• What are your feelings when looking at the artwork? Your written reflection?

Amanda's forest, Tabitha's brain, and Andrea's broken boat

Figures 7.1 and 7.2 illustrate patient representations of the mind. Amanda created a dense jungle, and discussed feeling lost, overwhelmed, and often scared (Figure 7.1). In the writing exercise, her peers noticed the lush vitality of the forest and vines wrapping and twisting around the trees. They imagined feeling awestruck, uncertain, and even disoriented if placing themselves in the image. Group members were curious about what other life forms existed in this jungle, and identified fear of what may be lurking in the thick undergrowth. One member shared that the twisting vines reminded him of neural networks of the brain, describing the landscape as complex and intricate. Amanda noted that her peers listed emotions similar to those she intended to express, and she reported feeling understood. Jon Allen often describes an interaction with a patient where he commented that the mind can be a scary place, and the patient replied, "Yes, I wouldn't want to go in there alone." We chose this image for the cover of this book because it seemed to depict this sentiment. In MBAT, art therapists and patients journey together through the potentially treacherous landscapes of the mind.

Figure 7.1. Amanda's internal landscape

In the next example, Tabitha constructed a collage, dividing her brain into sections (Figure 7.2). Her peers in the group were curious about the segmentation in the image. Tabitha reported feeling fragmented and experienced forgetfulness due to electroconvulsive therapy (ECT). The colorful sections of the mind represented memories that she was not able to access.

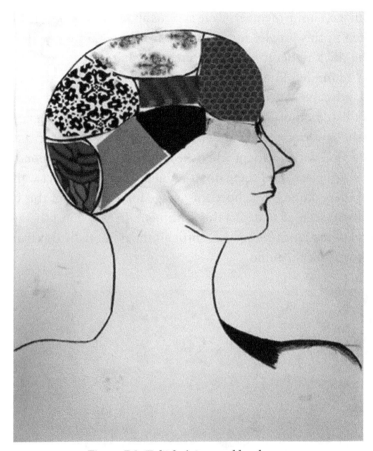

Figure 7.2. Tabitha's internal landscape

Andrea painted a boat with a broken mast (Figure 7.3). She described the boat as stuck and stagnant, noting that the ocean itself was not overpowering, but the boat was stuck there because of the broken mast. She described the night-time as both beautiful and ominous, as there was no one else around and she did not know how to get out. Andrea discussed difficulty connecting with people who did not have similar experiences, making a reference to her depression and recent suicide attempt. The image was described as peaceful, not uncomfortable. Both Andrea and her peers mentalized feeling trapped, stuck, and isolated. Her peers wondered about feeling terrified, and Andrea responded that this is not really a horrible place to be.

Figure 7.3. Andrea's internal landscape

Written responses to Bob's and Glenda's artwork

Figures 7.4 to 7.7 demonstrate the writing process that is often used after art making as a way to deepen the mentalizing process. The paper is folded or flipped over as necessary, so that each writer does not see what anyone else wrote. This allows each group member to respond independently and the art maker to receive each perspective separately, yet to notice whether there are common themes.

In Figure 7.4, Bob did a pencil drawing of a large figure with a zigzag line through a faceless head. The head is being held up by a mechanical support of some sort. Figure 7.5 is an example of the group writing process, with Bob's writing at the top followed by responses from his peers and both art therapists.

Figure 7.4. Bob's mind drawing

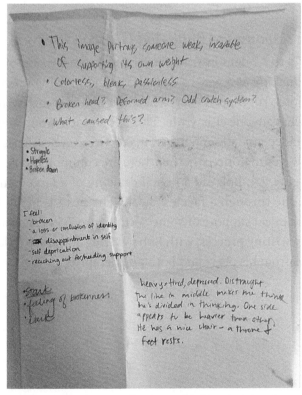

Figure 7.5. Written reflections of Bob's mind drawing

Bob wrote: This image portrays someone weak, incapable of supporting its own weight; colorless, bleak, passionless; broken head? Deformed art? Odd crutch system? What caused this?

Peer #1 writes: Struggle; hopeless; broken down.

Therapist #1: I feel: broken; a loss or confusion of identity; self-deprecation; reaching out for/needing support.

Therapist #2: Stark; feeling of brokenness; dark.

Peer #4: Heavy and tired, depressed. Distraught. The line in the middle makes me think he's divided in thinking. One side appears to be heavier than the other. He has a nice chair—a throne and feet rests.

Figure 7.6 is Glenda's drawing of her mind as a library. Figure 7.7 is another example of the group writing process.

Figure 7.6. Glenda's mind drawing

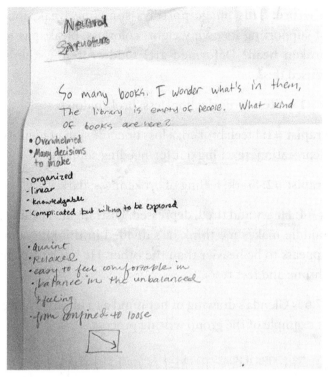

Figure 7.7. Written reflections of Glenda's mind drawing

Glenda writes: Neutral, structure.

Peer #1: So many books. I wonder what's in them. The library is empty of people. What kind of books are here?

Peer #2: Overwhelmed; many decisions to make.

Therapist #1: Organized; linear; knowledgeable; complicated but willing to be explored.

Therapist #2: Quaint; relaxed; easy to feel comfortable in; feeling balance in the unbalanced; from confined to loose.

These examples show how this writing process is a way for each group member to practice explicitly mentalizing every other group member as well as the art therapists. Each person writes a response from their own perspective or asks questions. It is up to each artist to decide what fits and what does not. They are able to receive feedback from multiple people about their artwork and what it expresses. This allows patients to see themes they did not consciously intend to communicate, and can help them come into contact with their thoughts and feelings. At times, patients share that they feel validated when written responses reflect how they feel or offer a new perspective. Patients have also reported feeling vulnerable or surprised when their peers accurately identify emotional content. Even when written perceptions do not fit with the artist's intentions, it offers an opportunity to be curious and to clarify, thus engaging the group in explicit mentalizing.

Understanding differing perspectives

Mental flexibility is an important component of mentalizing. It involves the ability to recognize and accept differing perspectives. Effective mentalizing is distinguished by several features, including perspective taking. According to Asen and Fonagy (2012, p.110), "perspective taking is characterized by the acceptance that the same phenomenon or process can look very different from different perspectives and that these tend to reflect each individual's different experiences and history." When patients can accept that the same event is experienced differently, they can break free of the assumption that their emotions are equivalent to those of others. Shifting perspectives takes heroic effort for some patients, used to operating from the belief that others think and feel as they do. Unexplored certainty about affective states in others is a source of interpersonal conflict for many patients with personality disorders. Instead of accepting these assumptions, the mentalizing group functions to help patients differentiate self and other. Each person's perspective is understood as valid, and the idea is to further explore differences to discover how they are connected to past and present experiences. The therapist models this by demonstrating acceptance of alternative perceptions. Mentalizing therapists use open curiosity about the minds of others to adjust, rework, and ultimately improve understanding (Allen *et al.* 2008; Asen and Fonagy 2012; Bateman and Fonagy 2016).

Art theme: Draw a sculpture

In the following art directive, *Draw a sculpture* (see Table 7.2), we move outside of the multipurpose room. The group gathers in an outdoor courtyard around a geometric metal sculpture, which they are invited to draw. Assorted types of charcoal (compressed, vine, pencil), erasers, paper, and drawing boards are provided. Patients are told that they may choose to sit anywhere around the sculpture, as long as group therapists can see them. Some sit close to the sculpture on a sidewalk or nearby bench. Others sit under the shade of a tree or on the grassy knoll, a little further away. The rather relentless Texas heat typically encourages rapid art making. The discussion, however, takes some time.

Upon return to the multipurpose room, drawings are attached to the whiteboard and the group members are invited into quiet observation. Discussion ensues as therapists may ask the group to identify similarities and differences among the collective art pieces (see Figure 7.8). A patient may be asked to identify a drawing other than his or her own to describe. The group members are asked questions about the image first, before the artist clarifies and shares about their process. Patients are invited to consider how past and present experiences and mental states might influence differing perspectives. Where people choose to sit in relation to the sculpture, how materials are applied, and formal elements such as the size, scale, and perspective of the drawings are also discussed in terms of what may drive the artist's decisions. This process demonstrates how the same subject can be viewed, understood, and interpreted differently. We make an explicit link to subjectivity in interpersonal contexts.

Table 7.2. Draw a sculpture

Description
• The group gathers around a sculpture in the courtyard. Patients are instructed to draw the sculpture. Materials are limited to charcoal, pencils, and paper.
• The group returns to the multipurpose room and drawings are placed on the whiteboard.
• Patients are reminded that this is not an art critique; rather, the purpose is to try and mentalize each other through the artwork, to think about what each image may communicate about its maker, and what the artist is communicating through the image.

Processing/discussion questions
• What is communicated in each image? How might the artist be feeling? What might this image reveal about the artist?
• What is it like to hear your peers' perspectives of your image? Is there anything you would like to clarify?
• What was it like to have art media and subject limitations?

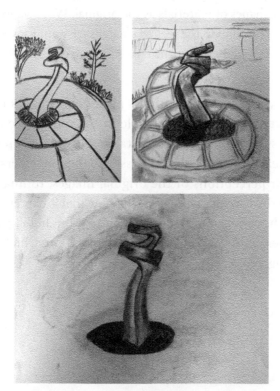

Figure 7.8. Examples of drawing a sculpture

Art theme: Response art

A second art prompt (see Table 7.3) used to foster appreciation for differing perspectives involves pre-existing works of art by artists with varying degrees of recognition. We selected about 30 images for our collection, which includes small prints, museum postcards, and printed photographs of both abstract and representational work ranging from prints of Willem de Kooning's *Woman 1* and Gustav Klimt's *The Kiss* to Banksy postcards and Wangechi Mutu collage images. We spread the art images around the table and invite patients to choose one that "stands out" to them, for whatever reason. We say,

> Perhaps you are familiar with the artwork, maybe it reminds you of something, or elicits a particular emotion. Once you have decided, we ask that you create your own art response to the chosen image. An art response is not a reproduction, though it can include similar colors or shapes or materials as the original. What we would like is for you to respond to the feeling elicited. We want for your artwork to reflect what it is about the chosen image that stands out to you or captivates you.

After the working phase, patients place their images beside the original artwork on a smaller table in the room. The therapists initiate a slow walk around the table with all group members observing each piece. During discussion, group members are asked about their perceptions of the original images, to imagine what captivated the patient's attention, and how that is expressed in their artwork. The variety of imagery and explanations highlight differing perspectives and invite curiosity and exploration, which is vital to mentalizing.

Table 7.3. Response art

Description
• Patients view a variety of art prints and are instructed to choose one that they connect with. Perhaps it sparks a memory, emotion, or curiosity; perhaps they identify with something in the image.
• Group members are then invited to create a response art piece, focusing on depicting what is evoked from the original artwork.
• Patients are reminded that response art is not a direct copy, though some elements of the original piece may present in their artwork (e.g., color, movement, shapes).
• Patients' artwork is displayed next to the originals and group members walk around to view each set. Discussion follows.
Processing/discussion questions
• How did you go about selecting your art print?
• What emotions, memories, questions, or thoughts were elicited from the original art? How did you decide to capture this in your response art?
• Looking at your peers' images, what reactions come up?
• What is it like to hear your peers' perspectives of your image? Is there anything you'd like to clarify?

Christie's floating figure

Christie, a 20-year-old patient, chose a Caitlin Hurd painting of a floating figure and created a response art piece to the emotion elicited from the original painting (Figure 7.9). She reported that it represented feeling numb, going through the motions of life passively. The group offered their observations about the nondescript face in the image. One patient wondered if it had something to do with not having an identity or not having a good understanding of who this person is. Another patient offered that maybe the piece is about losing someone because the figure appears to be stuck and parts of the image appear to be fading away. Another patient called attention to the "energy" of the marks/line work inside the body of the figure and near the head of the figure, in contrast to the lack of activity or detail in the face, and wondered if perhaps there was more going on inside the figure than what they portrayed externally. Yet another patient noticed the artist's rendering of the background, and was curious about the lack of detail in relation to this person's sense of belonging. The group imagined feeling: frozen, stuck, suspended, unknown, unknowable, uncertain, confused, alone, afraid. Christie discussed her response artwork, and shared that she has been living for others and not herself, doing what her family has wanted instead of making autonomous decisions.

Many of Christie's core issues stemmed from an insecure attachment style. She experienced relationships as threatening and people as controlling, unreliable, and critical. Her anger about feeling controlled was expressed by impulsive escalations of maladaptive coping behaviors, often putting her in dangerous situations. This, in turn, alerted those in her family and support system to attempt to further control her in order to keep her safe. Stuck in this dynamic, Christie was either the obedient, docile, "good" child, or the rebel without regard for herself. This image depicted the former, with the figure appearing to be in a motionless trance. Christie also struggled with feelings of shame and inadequacy, making it difficult for her to share her mind and interact with others. Her artwork reflected her past and current experiences, which influenced her interpretation of the original art image chosen.

Figure 7.9. Christie's response art

CHAPTER 8

Mentalizing about Treatment and Beyond

This chapter includes art prompts related to core issues, agency, and maintaining hope during and after treatment. We explore each concept, describe the corresponding art therapy directives, and provide examples of patient artwork and discussion.

Imagining core issues for treatment

What is a core issue?

A primary goal of brief treatment is to develop a working formulation of what is keeping the patient stuck. Core issues are a way to understand underlying barriers. For emerging adults facing a *failure to launch*, it is useful to uncover these barriers as they attempt to enter adult roles. In educational groups, specific distinctions are made between diagnoses and core issues. *Diagnoses* are presented as a way of categorizing psychiatric symptoms, providing useful shorthand for clinicians to communicate with one another. *Core issues* are described as the drivers for symptoms. They are more individualized and descriptive than diagnoses, which often do not capture the nuances of a person's unique set of circumstances.

The mentalizing treatment process is aimed at developing a narrative formulation of problems, conceptualized as a collaborative work in progress. The patient is central to this formulation and co-creates it with the treatment team. Compass patients are encouraged to consider questions pertaining to view of self, relationships/view of others, managing emotions, traumatic experiences, experiences of success/failure, and engagement in treatment (see Tables 8.1 and 8.2). These questions are explored in individual therapy and family therapy, and surface in interpersonal interactions with peers as the crux of milieu therapy. They help the patient to identify internal and external barriers to progress.

The patient's list of core issues is presented to the team and used in the formulation. The formulation is then offered to the patient for comment and refinement, which models the mentalizing approach. The list of core issues breaks down seemingly insurmountable problems into treatable pieces that may be more manageable. For the patient and providers, this process organizes thinking around treatment issues and shifts the focus to clearly stated goals. The formulation makes explicit links to aspects of treatment that will help the patient reach these goals (Allen *et al.* 2012; O'Malley 2018).

Table 8.1. Core issues: Questions to consider

View of self	How do I view myself? How well do I know, understand, accept myself?
	What are some of the core beliefs I have about myself?
	What are fears that I have about myself?
Relationships/ view of others	How do I view others? Do I feel known, understood, accepted by others?
	Do I see others as trustworthy, generally available, or able to meet my needs?
	What are some of the core beliefs I have about other people?
	What are fears that I have about relationships?
Managing emotions	What is my relationship with my emotions?
	Do I try to numb my emotions, suppress, or try to escape them?
	Do my emotions feel overwhelming and overpowering to the point that I struggle to manage them?
Traumatic experiences	Have I experienced trauma that has impacted my functioning, view of self, or others?
	What is the emotional impact of the trauma? How does it continue to affect me?

Experiences of success/failure	Do I feel capable of effecting change in my life?
	Do I have agency and autonomy to make decisions for myself? Do I fear that my independence will be taken from me or I will be abandoned if I show self-sufficiency?
	How do I approach problems? Is it easier to do nothing than to try?
	Do I self-sabotage when I have some experience of success?
Engagement in treatment	What motivations are driving my treatment? Am I getting treatment because it is something I want for myself or something that others want for me?
	Do I have hope that treatment will help?
	Are past treatment experiences impacting how I engage in treatment now?
	Am I generally confused about how treatment works?

Table 8.2. Pam's core issues[1]

View of self	Pam's early family environment seems to have contributed to an insecure attachment style. She may have experienced her caregivers as emotionally undependable or unavailable and feels herself as unworthy of close relationships.
	Shame impacts Pam's negative view of self and low confidence. She feels that she can never be good enough which makes it difficult for her to share her mind or interact with others.
Relationships/ view of others	An insecure attachment style creates challenges for Pam to trust others and feel safe in relationships.
	Pam has trouble maintaining close relationships. She feels scared that she will be abandoned or rejected and may preemptively reject others before they reject her for perceived weaknesses, which she tries to hide. This results in feeling isolated and lonely.
Managing emotions	When Pam feels controlled by her family, she responds with anger and impulsive action, which escalates her maladaptive coping behaviors, and in turn increases the family's attempts to control her.
	Pam seeks comfort in substances when people feel unsafe to her and she is unable to manage her feelings.
	Pam has challenges identifying and expressing her feelings, which contributes to a sense of disconnection.

cont.

---

1 Core issues are presented here in a table format for clarity; however, they are presented to patients in a list or narrative format.

Traumatic experiences	In addition to unmet attachment needs in early childhood, Pam has a recent history of sexual trauma. She may be at higher risk for the recurrence of such events when under the influence of substances. While substance use may serve as a means to escape from difficult emotions, use becomes dangerous for her safety and further contributes to her shame.
Experiences of success/failure	Pam struggles with perfectionism, which often shows up as procrastination and avoidance. Her feeling of inadequacy contributes to difficulty beginning tasks and participating in class as well as relationships. Despite these challenges, Pam has graduated high school, obtained admission to a college of her choice, and completed 3 semesters. Pam is motivated to complete her degree.
Engagement in treatment	Pam is hardworking and creative, maintaining honesty and collaboration throughout the treatment process. She has demonstrated willingness and motivation for change. Though she has difficulty feeling connected to others, her peers seem to view her as a leader and role model in the milieu.

How does art help clarify core issues?

As previously stated, a mentalizing framework does not use artwork as a diagnostic tool. MBT, in fact, places little emphasis on narrative content. Instead, the focus rests on the mentalizing process (Bateman and Fonagy 2012a). Yet, because brief treatment settings place particular importance on diagnostic formulation, some attention to content is warranted. The mentalizing process is the means by which the patient and treatment team collaboratively arrive at a comprehensive formulation. The aim is to capture the patient's unique experiences and the team's experience of the patient.

Mentalizing is an art, not a math equation. It takes time and talent to develop a formulation that fits; or, as Allen and colleagues note, "no algorithm is available for finding the proper focus. Our focus on mentalizing is intended merely to increase the odds of the patient and therapist conjointly getting it right" (2012, pp.190–191). In the same way, the art therapy group provides an avenue for the patient and treatment providers to collaboratively develop a formulation that is a good fit. Art therapy helps patients to explore and share their minds with others safely. Patients externalize feelings, thoughts, and fantasies, and work through them symbolically. This seems more tolerable than verbal expression for many young adults on Compass, especially those who were referred to the MBAT group because they were not able to explore issues in other areas of treatment. Art therapy allows them to gradually portray dilemmas and to work through them visually. Additionally, deficits in mentalizing may present during the art therapy process.

Art theme: Stuck place

Several art prompts are offered in the MBAT group that focus on core issues. The first is the *Stuck place* directive (see Table 8.3). In the MBAT group, patients are invited to create an image representing a place where they feel stuck. The majority of the time is used for this task. Toward the end of the allotted art-making time, patients are asked to alter the image to make it feel a little less stuck. They are offered suggestions of adding something, taking something away, or introducing a new material. For patients who find it challenging to change the image, the option to create a separate image is offered (keeping in mind time limitations). The patients are then invited to share their artwork with the group, describing the original artwork and the alteration.

Table 8.3. Stuck place

Description
• Create an image representing a place where you feel stuck.
• Alter the image to make it feel a little less stuck.
Processing/discussion questions
• Describe the process of creating your image. What did you start with and what did you change?
• What was it like when you were asked to alter the artwork?
• How did you decide what to add or take away?
• What is it like for you right now, looking at the image? What feelings, thoughts, or questions arise?

Jack's stuck place

This art directive brings to surface core issues and also illuminates mentalizing capacity and deficits. For example, Figure 8.1 depicts Jack's image of his stuck place. Jack began by drawing a hand dispensing medication into an open mouth, with pills falling out of the intestine. He then added crying eyes and a bleeding heart, with blood dripping from the bottom. The black abyss at the base of the page was described as a receptacle for the pills, tears, and blood. Jack stated that "nothing was working" and he was stuck because of seemingly futile attempts to relieve his suffering. When invited to alter the image, Jack added a stopper/cork at the end of the intestinal tube. Next, he drew a Band-Aid on the heart, though it did not appear to be covering the source of the drip. The final addition was a small fairy holding and kissing the eye to "make it better," according to Jack.

During discussion, Jack acknowledged his search for "quick fixes" to resolve problems, which at times manifested in treatment as medication-seeking behavior. Some group members related to Jack, and several demonstrated curiosity about external sources of relief. Jack spoke about the futility of the actions taken to resolve the distress. The pills were initially falling into an abyss, fairies do not exist, and the Band-Aid was applied ineffectually. A group member asked, "Whose hand is holding the pills?" and another expressed curiosity about the fairy. Jack responded by describing the fairy as a representation of magical thinking, and identified a rather unhelpful view he held that things could improve with little effort on his part. He supposed that this was why his alterations to the image involved action from external sources. Jack's image is demonstrative of *teleological thinking*, characterized by the reduction of mental states to tangible action. As previously discussed, in this nonmentalizing mode, feelings can only be expressed by observable behavior or understood by physical causes. For example, *if you do not answer my call, then you do not love me*; *you bumped into me so you must want to hurt me*; or in this case, *a Band-Aid, kiss from a fairy, or pills from a doctor will make it all better.*

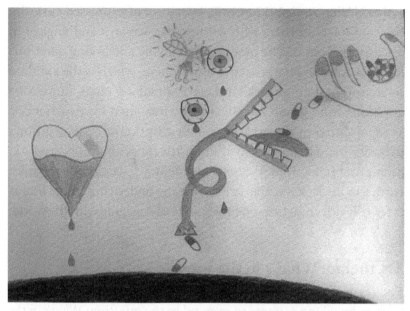

Figure 8.1. Jack's stuck place

Group members then turned their attention to the fragmentation in Jack's image. They wondered about the detached body parts, floating eyes, mouth, heart, and hand from an unknown origin. They wondered about the lack of connection of these parts to a whole person or form. Jack responded that he had not given it much thought, but perhaps this reflected how disconnected he felt from himself.

This drawing was created after several weeks in treatment, and Jack noted that he had come to realize his responsibility in the treatment process. He found this difficult to remember in times of intense emotional pain, when he is more inclined to demand immediate solutions. Jack had some awareness of an urgency to act quickly to mitigate his distress and heavy reliance on external action as validation for his suffering. His artwork seemed to further underline his expressed difficulty with a teleological mode of thinking, which interfered with his mentalizing ability in interpersonal contexts.

The MBAT group provides a space for patients to "think together" (Allen *et al.* 2012, p.187), by nature of expressed curiosity from interested others who witness the artwork and engage in discussion about it. The process of clarifying and asking questions fosters a collaborative reflective atmosphere, which is the antidote to nonmentalizing. Jack's image seemed to elicit numerous questions from group members as we imagined his experiences, as represented in the artwork and description of it. The group's curiosity increased Jack's own inquisitiveness about his artwork, prompting reflectiveness about his mental state and core issues. Furthermore, Jack was able to examine the underlying causes for his externally driven, action-oriented mode of engaging with the world.

Art theme: What's in the way?

The second art prompt (see Table 8.4) helps identify issues and barriers by asking patients to respond to the question: *What's in the way?* During discussion, group members are invited to imagine what it would feel like to be in the image or how it would feel to embody various components of the image, for example a tree or a figure in the corner.

Table 8.4. What's in the way?

Description
• Use the art materials to respond to the question: *What's in the way?*
• Consider past and present barriers from internal and external sources.
Processing/discussion questions
• Describe the process of creating your image.
• What is it like hearing from your peers and seeing their artwork?
• What would it feel like to be the _____ in this image?
• What is it like for you right now, looking at the artwork? What feelings, thoughts, or questions arise?

Brandon's barriers

Brandon was an emerging adult patient who came to Compass following a failed attempt at college and ongoing conflict with his family. He struggled with mental flexibility and was fairly combative with and devaluing of staff and other patients. The team's initial impression of Brandon was that he employed narcissistic defenses, making it extremely difficult to connect with others meaningfully.

Brandon was referred to the MBAT group and shared his art response to this prompt (see Figure 8.2). Brandon was true to form in his tongue-and-cheek description of the image, jokingly calling attention to the phallic nature of the turnips and placement of the water hose. Brandon described himself in the image, attempting to water a field of extraordinarily large turnips. He explained that the hose was too short to reach and did not expel enough water; he was thus ill equipped.

A few group members followed along in jest, but when the laughter subsided, Brandon demonstrated some vulnerability by sharing his deep-rooted feelings of inadequacy. He spoke openly about how he gets in his own way. His peers offered feedback that they were not aware of Brandon's experience of himself as inadequate because he presented in groups as confident and self-assured. The group discussion also highlighted Brandon's use of humor and sarcasm to distance himself from painful emotions and from other people. Brandon began to make sense of these difficulties in the relational context of the group.

Figure 8.2. What's in the way?

Agency

The concept of agency is part of the Compass motto. Every week during a community meeting, staff and patients sit together in a large circle to exchange information and discuss community issues. At the opening of this patient-led meeting, the Compass motto is recited: *ARCH—Agency, Respect, Compassion, Honesty*. A common charge among staff and patients alike is, "take agency in treatment."

Agency refers to the ability to take responsibility for actions. It comprises a person's capacity to act independently, make choices, and initiate action toward a purpose or desired goal. When a person has a sense of self that is cohesive, is able to make choices, and to be accountable for those choices, they are taking agency (Allen *et al.* 2003; O'Malley 2018). In the context of treatment, agency is demonstrated when patients have a vested interest in being an active part of the process. They are willing to examine their actions and take ownership for their contributions to problems. This is in contrast to the belief that simply showing up is sufficient for treatment to be effective.

Some patients enter Compass with a passive mindset of having treatment *done to them* by all-knowing, benevolent treatment providers, wizards behind a magical curtain. Others believe that the treatment team is inept, dispensable, and that they might as well *go it alone*. Neither view is helpful. The goal is collaboration, and mentalizing is the means by which that is achieved. Mentalizing requires and promotes agency. It is the foundation for a sense of identity and self-awareness. Mentalizing challenges perceptions that events simply happen *to* people; rather, people have ownership of their behavior and ability to effect change (Allen *et al.* 2003). When we encourage agency in treatment, we want patients to feel a shared responsibility and belief that their contributions are valued and impactful to the outcome.

Agency in emerging adulthood

The transition from adolescence to adulthood is difficult for many young people. The addition of psychiatric disorders or substance abuse further impedes successful navigation of adult roles. Many Compass patients face this challenge. They seem to have missed the exit on the road to adulthood and are stuck on a perpetual highway loop, propelled by an inability to gain an integrated and cohesive sense of self. At times these young adults cannot hold a view of self as agentive of change. They typically have issues with attachment, and demonstrate highly dependent, enmeshed relationships with their parents—anger, resentment, low self-confidence, and acting out are common consequences in these parent–child relationships. In emerging adulthood, young people must work through conflicts around gaining autonomy, while concurrently forming and re-forming connections in various relational contexts (Poa 2006).

Agency in art therapy

The act of making art promotes agency, as patients are required to make decisions about materials and application. Art therapy quite possibly offers a sense of agency and control in ways that verbalizing simply cannot. For some patients, talking about dilemmas can perpetuate a self-perception as a victim, helpless and powerless, or playing assigned roles. Others may perceive that they have enormous power to impact or control others. In art therapy, however, people are in charge of what they create, without severe impact on others. Art making encourages authorship as patients produce art objects reflecting their experiences.

Additionally, the artwork develops as a second order representation, a version of reality but not reality itself. Springham and Huet (2018, p.5) describe this *as if* quality of the artwork, noting, "differentiation from reality allows for experimentation in thought, which facilitates the change to imagine possibilities without the terror of damaging actual reality." In this way, patients in the art therapy group have the unique opportunity to play with reality using art materials. They can take a step back from difficult situations, examine them from the outside in, and imagine various scenarios without fear of consequences.

For example, Tom, a patient who struggled to locate agency within himself, was given a realistic sense of agency in the art therapy group. While speaking about his dilemmas, he perceived himself as either helpless, inadequate, and passively experiencing life, or inordinately powerful, with great capacity to impact others. These roles were assigned to him early on by his parents. His mother felt he could do nothing without her, and his father dismissed his struggles to preserve his view of a successful son who could do anything. In art therapy, Tom was in charge of what he created without any serious impact on others or on either parent's view of him. He could make decisions, play with reality, and express feelings without fear of getting out of control. The safety of the art therapy space provides opportunities for patients to take agency.

Art theme: Life as a book

The art theme focusing on agency is described in Table 8.5. In this MBAT group, patients are asked to design a book cover for a story about their life.

Table 8.5. Life as a book

Description
• Consider your life as a book. Choose a title to reflect the strengths and vulnerabilities of the main character and a central theme and conflict in the book. Create a book cover using art materials.
• Write the blurb for the book, a brief description of what others will read on the back cover to pique interest in the book.
Processing/discussion questions
• Describe the process of creating your image.
• How does your book cover reflect your experiences?
• How do your peers' book covers reflect your understanding of each person?
• What is the genre of book (e.g., thriller, romance, suspense, adventure, sci-fi)?
• What would it be like to live in that story?

The following examples illustrate patient responses to this task.

Joe's and Sheila's book covers

Joe's book was titled *Give It a Shot... Or Don't*. The cover depicted a figure lying in bed in a dark room, thinking about the outside world (Figures 8.3 and 8.4). His book blurb read:

> *Give It a Shot... Or Don't* is a seminal landmark of contemporary fiction. Set in Florida between the early nineties and modern day, it outlines in meticulous detail the life of a young man struggling to define himself. With little entertainment value, it is a mystery how this novel became published or received any recognition.

> "A great read before bed—perfect for putting you to sleep." —The New York Times

> "Very hard to relate to, but I would recommend to someone upon which you wish to exact revenge."—*Miami Herald*

> "Don't bother finishing. The first chapter alone is enough to make you value your quality of life a little more."—*The New Yorker*

> WINNER OF THE PULITZER PRIZE

> OPRAH'S BOOK CLUB

> About the Author

> ...resides in Florida where, like this protagonist, he struggles between meandering and floundering. He has two cats.

Joe faced the dilemma of ambivalence—to do or not, to try or not, to take action or not. Group discussion of Joe's book cover exposed a tension between failure and success, agency and powerlessness, ever-present for many emerging adults. His peers called attention to the contrast between the denigrating commentaries written about the book and the awards received. This led to a discussion on Joe's drive for success and perfection coupled with his inability to take action toward goals, which was the crux of his stuckness.

Figure 8.3. Joe's life as a book: Front cover

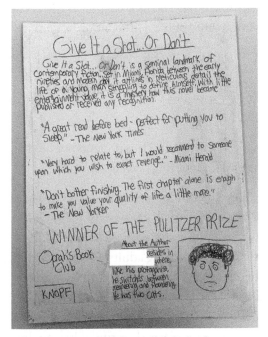

Figure 8.4. Joe's life as a book: Back cover

Sheila created a book cover for her life story, *The Other:* a blank page with only the title written in the bottom right corner. She explained to the group that she sees herself as the unknowable other. The group commented on the blankness of the image, the open space, and the minimalist lettering. Sheila spoke about religious, racial, and sexual identities that made her feel other and isolated in her family and community. She noted that she tries to present a blank slate when she meets new people, not revealing too much about herself. Sheila recognized that the blank space leaves it open for others to project onto her and make assumptions that are usually not accurate. She then feels misunderstood and further isolated.

Maintaining hope

Much of how we conceptualize the role of hope in treatment is based on the work of Jon Allen, who speaks and writes fluently on the topic. Oftentimes, our patients arrive to treatment in dismal conditions: following suicide attempts, with severe trauma histories and debilitating barriers to functioning at a desired level. The concept of hope may seem alien to the hopeless, yet making room for discussions about hope uncovers far more than the extent to which people have given up. Patients often reveal sparks of resilience and expose unrecognized motivators, existing even in the presence of grave despair and uncertainty.

While emerging adulthood is described as the age of possibilities, full of optimism and hope for the future (Arnett 2000b), emerging adults grappling with mental health issues may have a different experience. Hopelessness often stems from a fixed certainty about the permanence of their struggles and impedes their ability to see possibilities; those with minimal success in navigating adult roles and spaces may have a narrowing field of vision for the future. So the topic of hope is particularly useful for these individuals, offering perspective and creating awareness of previously unseen potential.

Allen (2013) notes the importance of distinguishing a *hope* from a *wish*. He writes: "Wishing is easy; maintaining hope is hard. Wishing can be unrealistic; hope must not be. Wishing is passive;

hope is active. Wishing can be a means of escaping reality; hope entails facing reality" (2013, p.246). A wish is often directed toward objects of desire, yet hoping moves beyond this. Hope is also different from optimism, as it is "too lighthearted a word to capture what is needed in the oftentimes-grueling process of healing from trauma" (Allen 2013, p.247).

Art theme: Maintaining hope

We believe that art making facilitates movement toward hope. The imaginative quality of mentalizing and hoping becomes a physical process in art therapy. Patients must utilize their imaginations and begin to visualize possibilities in order to create artwork reflecting hope.

At the beginning of the *Maintaining hope* group (see Table 8.6) time is spent discussing hope as a foundation for treatment. Hope requires agency to take steps forward in the presence of uncertainty, tolerance for fear and doubt, realistic expectations, and a willingness to imagine a different future. Attachment relationships offer a source of *borrowed hope*; hope from family, friends, and therapists sustains patients who are in despair. When the lens of depression blocks a person's vision of a realistic future, others may be able to see what they cannot (Allen 2013; Groat and Allen 2013). In the MBAT group, patients identify people who hold hope for them. They also acknowledge that doubt is often coupled with hope, and discuss what gives them hope. Following this discussion, patients are invited to create an image of hope.

Table 8.6. Maintaining hope

Description
• The group discusses hope and develops a working definition.
• Patients are invited to create an image reflecting hope.
• Art making may be followed by a written reflection on the artwork.
• Patients then share and discuss their artwork, noting similar themes in the images.

Processing/discussion questions
- What was it like to create an image of hope?
- How did you choose to visualize hope?
- What do you connect with as you look at your peers' images? Are there similarities? Differences?
- What thoughts or emotions come up as you look at your image? Your peers' images? What are your feelings when looking at the artwork? Your written reflection?

Kelly's pockets of light

We often see hope in the progression of the tangible art artifacts patients create during their time in treatment. Kelly described her final image (see Figure 8.5) in her last MBAT group after several months of hospitalization.

Kelly: This whole time, all this dark stuff on the side is fear and hopelessness. It's what I've been feeling for so long, and recently there have been some pockets of light, like feeling alive or little moments of feeling lighter. But it's surrounded by fear and hopelessness, these feelings of being trapped. But it's better than having no light or no pockets. I'm trying to figure it out and where I am in my treatment is recognizing that there can be two things—there can be fear and there can also be hope at the same time. I can be afraid and I can also do something. So they both exist.

Therapist: What is it like when you have those moments of lightness?

Kelly: I think it's more noticeable because I felt so afraid and hopeless for so long, so these moments where I can feel anything but that—and feel this warmth and life—are that much more noticeable and that much better because it's been gone for so long. In a way it's kind of something that I needed to experience to see that all of it's worth it. Because I felt like I was just trudging along, just working to exist even though it's miserable. Now I'm working to exist because I want to.

Figure 8.5. Kelly's hope

These poignant statements resonated, as Kelly was generally rigid in her thinking. She acknowledged early on having black-and-white thinking, and would often become stuck in a black hole of despair, pulling in anyone who dared to come close. The lightness she described in her artwork was nothing short of radical. It was a reflection of significant shifts in thinking and movement toward mental flexibility.

Hope for the helpers

Therapists need to maintain hope too. Karl Menninger emphasized the importance of stimulating "the right amount of hope—some, but not too much. Excess of hope is a presumption and leads to disaster. Deficiency of hope is despair and leads to decay" (as cited in Allen 2003, p.247).

In my first year on Compass, I vividly remember a supervision meeting conducted in the spaces between my sobs. I felt uncertain about the work and my role in it. I was arrested with an overwhelming sense of futility. I recall saying to my supervisor "it's too much. The hopelessness, it's catching." After listening attentively and offering validation and tissues for the deluge pouring from my face, my supervisor asked a question not easily forgotten: "What are your expectations, Kula?" (Personal reflection)

This question points to the therapist's task of maintaining hope that is also realistic. In this case, the sense of feeling overwhelmed stemmed from a pressure to help, to know, to effect change and quickly. We imagine this sense of omnipotence is common for new therapists and still, even seasoned therapists face challenges developing sound expectations for each patient. Allen (2013, p.248) writes:

> But knowing how much to expect is never easy. Cultivating hope is most difficult when patients express suicidal despair... How often I hear, "I'm exhausted." "I feel like giving up." "I can't keep fighting." "I want it to end." I bring to mind patients who have felt this way, continued the struggle, and been glad they did. This experience prevents me from joining patients in their wish to give up.

Early on, we recall few experiences of patients who were able to see a way out of the struggle. More accurately, we did not grasp the full measure of importance in acknowledging and appreciating these instances. We often felt hesitant to discuss hope, fearing it would open a Pandora's box of despair. As such, our hopelessness mirrored the patients, and we also lacked the ability to visualize a way out, feeling *caught* in the surrounding hopelessness. Through discussion with each other, colleagues, and supervisors, we began developing sound expectations not only for our patients, but also for ourselves. As therapists, we encourage patients to *borrow hope* from others. How easily we overlook our need to do the same.

Writing (and riding) on hope

At times, we invite patients to write about hope. Examples from previous patients include:

Hope.
From darkness there is light
The absence of despair
A four-letter word with a million meanings
A theory of some sort
Tangible yet fleeting
Yes, I like this word
Hope has saved me
From a villain so destructive
Myself.

Hope is the wide-open space of possibilities. It is not contained to this earth alone but will spread as far as you can see. Even when you seem to be lost in the darkness far above, there are still glimmers of hope all round you, shining through the void as beacons reaching out to you, beckoning you to persist through the seemingly endless darkness with the promise of a better existence. (For the corresponding image to this, see Figure 4.6 in Chapter 4.)

Hope is small and fleeting.
Hope has two legs on the ground.
Hope isn't waterproof, but still it rains.
Hope reads the warning signs.
Hope looks right, looks left.
Hope walks quietly forward.

A patient in the MBAT group created an abstract painting to reflect hope. Using a large sheet of paper, she took great care filling the page with various shades of blue. She remained intently focused on this process during the working phase of the group, not once looking up from her paper, paints, or brushes. She shared her reflective writing during group discussion. It was something like this:

Hope is a fragile thing, a pool of blue.
Sometimes filled to the brim, spilling over with plenty to give.
At other times, mere drops in a vast, deep pit.
Today, there is sufficient hope. Drawn from within, from without.
Some deep internal reserve kept hidden away
In case of drought.

This writing brilliantly encapsulates the hope of treatment—the building up of reserves, experiences of connection, moments of understanding, and being understood; the offering up and taking in, *in case of drought*. May we all have the courage to give and receive hope.

CHAPTER 9

Life of the Image

After the group, the image lives on. Artwork created in art therapy often resurfaces in other areas of treatment. It has proven a helpful informer for the treatment team, a valuable aid for the patient, and a powerful facilitator of the mentalizing process. While patients have full ownership of their artwork, they are informed at the start that the artwork is part of their treatment record. Patient artwork may be discussed in team meetings, clinical rounds, and diagnostic conferences; however, verbal permission is typically requested prior to showing a patient's art. Patients may initiate sharing their artwork, requesting to take it to individual therapy, team rounds, and family therapy.

Because the artwork is stored in folders in a locked cabinet in a locked room, patients are required to ask to take a piece with them. The art therapist then has the opportunity to ask about the patient's intentions. Most often patients respond by stating that if someone on their team or in their family could see the image, it may provide a better understanding of some aspect of the patient's experience. There are times when the art therapist will encourage the patient to take a piece with them to individual therapy or to a family session. In these instances it is always the patient's choice, and the art therapist is transparent about why it was suggested. Typically, patients are made aware that the artwork could provide a window to their experience and generate a dialogue. It may facilitate more transparency in how the patient shares their experiences with the team; for instance, the artwork may communicate the intensity of an emotion when a patient finds it hard to express verbally.

This chapter highlights how the image resurfaces in other areas of treatment, including treatment team interactions such as team meetings, clinical rounds, diagnostic conferences, family work, and individual therapy. First, though, we review the nature and functions of a mentalizing treatment team.

The mentalizing treatment team

Essential characteristics of a cohesive, well-functioning mentalizing treatment team include: commonality of purpose, respect for self and others, development and adherence to treatment plans, maintaining healthy team morale, and effective leadership. Regular communication among team members, flexibility in the team's process of defining goals, and maintaining consistency among team members are also important (Bales and Bateman 2012; Bateman and Fonagy 2016; Bateman and Krawitz 2013).

Karterud and Bateman (2012, pp.83–84) note the many benefits and challenges of a team approach when working with patients with a personality disorder:

> MBT takes a team approach, acknowledging that difficult-to-treat borderline patients will commonly engage several therapists in different aspects of treatment. The advantages of the team approach are that heavy responsibilities and countertransferences are shared by several people and that different perspectives on intricate problems supplement and enrich one another. The risk is that different and competing perspectives among different therapists may increase the possibility of destructive enactments of the patient's internal drama. The MBT format thus presupposes that therapists share the same theoretical position and that procedures exist for frequent exchange of information between the therapists.

Here, we focus on the utility of artwork to enhance mentalizing in team interactions. When patient artwork is present in team meetings, clinical rounds, and diagnostic conferences, it serves as a focal point, uniting the team's thinking about the patient and facilitating cohesiveness and unity. When team members view a patient's artwork, they reconnect with the patient's perspective. Looking at the artwork is a sensory experience that fosters empathy in the face of compassion fatigue.

Art in team meetings

At The Menninger Clinic, treatment teams meet weekly to discuss patient progress in treatment, goals, and safety concerns. Each discipline is present at the team meetings and team members speak about their experiences with the patient. When the patient's artwork is reviewed during the team meetings, the general consensus from team members is that the art promotes empathy and understanding. Artwork helps clarify the team's mind about the patient, especially where a general feeling of confusion persists. While patients may reveal different parts of self to different team members, when the entire team is looking at a piece of art, they are looking at the same thing together, seeing the patient through the window of their artwork.

For instance, Damien informed his treatment team in clinical rounds about his readiness to be discharged early and to a lower level of care, despite a clear recommendation from the team for him to stay the course of treatment and to attend a residential treatment center following discharge. The treatment team felt puzzled but had difficulty identifying specific sources of discomfort with Damien's plan. In team meetings, the uneasiness was palpable, an unwanted guest at the conference table that could not be named or spoken to. This was likely because, on the surface, Damien was going through the motions of treatment.

This facade crumbled during Damien's last week of hospitalization. Damien's group participation declined, though he did selectively attend some programming including the MBAT group. During his final art therapy session, he created a drawing of himself in the center of the page with a smaller figure floating above him saying the word "don't." One half of the image was light and the other side was dark. In the dark half of the image, Damien drew drugs, alcohol, and drug paraphernalia. To his credit, he was open during the group as he explained that he saw himself headed for relapse: "It feels like I am watching it happen outside of my body and there is nothing I can do to stop it." Damien's peers offered support and were encouraged to reflect on what it might feel like to be either figure in the image. The group mentalized about feeling frustrated, hopeless, and lacking control. One peer added that the dark side of the image seemed to have won already, as it took up more space. The group members were curious about Damien's feeling of powerlessness, and several peers expressed genuine concern.

The art therapist echoed the group's concern for Damien, and encouraged him to share the image with his treatment team. He declined to do so, but agreed to the art therapist taking the drawing to the treatment team. The artwork was brought to a team meeting where the team was in discussion about Damien's abrupt decision to discharge. At this point, the unwanted guest was given a face and a name that could be spoken: imminent relapse. Apprehension was expressed to Damien by the treatment team and his parents, who ultimately decided to support his decision in order for him to take ownership of the outcome. He soon left treatment, and relapsed within days.

In this example, the artwork provided a visual aid for the team to clarify their experiences of the patient. While individually several team members felt uneasy, the presence of Damien's art made tangible the source of this anxiety, and provided an impetus for the team to discuss these concerns openly. The creation of this artwork was the first time Damien expressed any doubts about his discharge and the possibility of relapse. He was then able to voice his concerns to the group; quite possibly the art therapy process clarified concerns that he had not taken the time to recognize. Additionally, he was aware that what was shared in the group would be brought back to the treatment team. The powerlessness expressed by Damien in relation to relapse mirrored the team's own powerlessness about his hasty decision to terminate treatment prematurely. While the artwork did not change the immediate outcome, it offered some preparation for the team, Damien's parents, and Damien, who had the courage to return to treatment shortly after his relapse.

Art in clinical rounds

Clinical rounds have been described as a "mentalizing extravaganza" (Allen *et al.* 2003, p.13). The patient meets with treatment team members to coordinate the treatment process, share observations and concerns, and participate in treatment planning. Each individual brings a unique perspective to engage in the process of mentalizing. Clinical rounds offer the space for understanding as well as misunderstanding, which sets the stage for mentalizing. From a mentalizing stance, the team members and patients are called to demonstrate mental flexibility, in order to consider various perspectives and possibilities to arrive at a shared understanding.

Sarah was in treatment for two weeks when she decided to bring a drawing to clinical rounds (see Figure 9.1). In the MBAT group, she drew four quadrants representing healthy and unhealthy thoughts and feelings. The top left reflected healthy thoughts, which she described as organized in a grid, with order, cohesion, and logic. The top right reflected unhealthy thoughts; this included a spiral, which she stated was a metaphor for ruminations that build upon each other and spin out of control. The bottom left quadrant was an image of healthy feelings. She noted that some feelings stood out more than others, but none felt too overwhelming. The bottom right of the drawing represented unhealthy feelings: chaotic, intense, difficult to make sense of, and blurred together. After sharing her artwork, Sarah's peers expressed surprise that Sarah experienced thoughts and feelings so intensely. They noted a seemingly pleasant, calm, and happy presentation. Sarah acknowledged a tendency to withhold difficulties from others, for fear of overwhelming them or being perceived as a burden. Sarah's peers also recognized the overall organization of her image, where even the chaos and struggle were contained by neatly drawn squares. Recognizing that she is only able to show a small piece of her emotions to her team, she expressed a desire to take her artwork to clinical rounds: "I wish my team could see this. I just want to give this to them and say 'this is my brain!'"

*Figure 9.1. Sarah's grid representing healthy and
unhealthy thoughts and feelings*

Sarah believed that the artwork would help the team to better understand her experiences as she often felt fearful of being misunderstood by others. She acknowledged that she was withholding emotional difficulties from the team, afraid of "being a burden." This dynamic kept the team in a bind: on the one hand, Sarah's thoughts of being burdensome prevented her from being more transparent. On the other hand, she felt frustration when the team struggled to understand or anticipate her needs. She expressed concern that treatment would be a waste of time. The team had a sense that they were missing something. Sarah could not speak her mind, which led to misunderstanding. She then expressed her anger passively and indirectly while smiling and placating when face-to-face. This incited frustration in those who interacted with her, and this pattern seemed present in her relationships outside of treatment.

When Sarah decided to take her drawing with her to team clinical rounds, the focus shifted as the artwork opened the dialogue for Sarah to explore the function of withholding in and out of treatment. When asked by the art therapists what it was like to show her artwork in clinical rounds, Sarah reported that she felt more understood. She stated that it was helpful to have a visual representation to show the team while she described her experience.

Like many patients, Sarah viewed her art as an impetus for understanding. The thinking suggested is: *if they can see it, they can feel some of what I feel, and they will understand.* While mistrust may prevent patients from open communication, art is a way of re-opening trust. Sarah's diagrammatic image served as an aid to communicating experiences and feelings that were already known to her, but that were difficult for her to share with the team. Talking about the image seemed to ease the process of discussion, while also arousing feelings in Sarah. Perhaps she felt she could speak more easily to the team about these feelings because she had externalized them in the image and experienced the group's mentalizing efforts. Perhaps the image itself eased the process of sharing her mind with others, because creating it in the first place was a sort of sharing of the mind. In any case, Sarah's drawing provided a concrete object, a focal point for her and for the team to observe together.

Art in diagnostic formulation

Treatment includes a number of comprehensive assessments conducted by members of different professional disciplines to clarify psychiatric disorders. Prior to the diagnostic process, team members share information frequently to update understanding of the patient's issues and progress. As such, understanding of the patient evolves over the weeks of treatment and assessment (Allen *et al.* 2003; The Menninger Clinic 2014). The diagnostic conference serves as a formal review, establishing working diagnoses, co-creating a list of core issues with the patient, and making recommendations for continued treatment. During the diagnostic conference, team members share assessment findings and perceptions in order to form a comprehensive picture of the patient and their issues. Each patient is also invited to create a list of core issues (Allen *et al.* 2012;

O'Malley 2018), detailing their understanding of what keeps them unable to function in a desired way and stuck from moving in the direction of their choice.

The artwork provides visual information to help the treatment team understand the patient's experiences and mentalizing capacity. The therapist's responsibility is to see the world through the patient's eyes and to validate their experience. Artwork adds to that process by providing a window into the patient's world. The mentalizing therapist's role is to understand, and art helps to make that possible. While artwork can help inform, illustrate, and underline the patient's experience, we want to stress that art therapy generates mental health, and in our clinical structure, the artwork is not in and of itself diagnostic of mental illness.

In diagnostic conferences, art brokers the experience of the patient who is not present during the initial diagnostic conference. The patient's voice is heard through the artwork, not filtered through reports and observations of others. The art serves as a physical representation of the patient's emotional experience (Wadeson 2010). Art can propel patients to emotional connection and understanding of self and others. Similarly, it encourages the treatment team to move beyond intellectual processing to deeper— oftentimes more empathic—understanding of the patient.

Figure 9.2 depicts the negative self-thoughts of a patient who struggled with self-harm and disordered eating. This image was presented in the patient's diagnostic conference as a representation of the constant stream of negative self-talk exploding from her mind and surrounding her. The patient explained that she felt trapped and unable to escape self-critical thoughts, which impeded relationships and impacted her interaction with the external environment. In the diagnostic conference, the team discussed the eruption of thoughts emanating from the head of the figure to form a barrier around her, and the hands drawn over her face, blocking the figure's view of what was happening around her. The body image issues, shame, eating disorder, and self-harm that the patient was struggling with were also visible in her drawing. Up to that point in treatment, the patient had seemed willfully avoidant of addressing salient issues she brought with her to treatment. The image helped the team to grasp the gravity of these problems and the patient's experience of being overwhelmed by them, not entirely avoidant of them. While she was hard to reach and engage in many ways, the artwork depicted many of the patient's core issues, which helped the team to clarify and refine their understanding of her. In effect, the team's language shifted from *she's not really willing to work on anything* to *she feels so overwhelmed by these issues coming from within, surrounding her, and threatening envelopment, that it is difficult to look at them.* Recovery of empathy is a common outcome when artwork is present.

Figure 9.2. Negative self-thoughts

A primary reason for admission to the hospital is to gain comprehensive diagnostic clarity, but that does not change how scary it can feel for patients with high epistemic vigilance to be observed, evaluated, and discussed. One patient illustrated her anxiety about the diagnostic process in the MBAT group (see Figure 9.3). She drew the team on one side of the page and herself looking at them as they discussed her diagnosis. Fears of feeling judged, pitied, labeled, dismissed, or invalidated prevailed as the patient expressed her concerns. This patient was fairly new to treatment, so the artwork provided an opportunity to clarify what the diagnostic process entailed. When all goes well and with a healthy working alliance, the patient sits with the team looking at the issues together.

Figure 9.3. Diagnostic conference drawing

Art in other spaces

When there are time limitations in the MBAT group, patients are able to continue processing their artwork in other areas of treatment. In addition to meetings where multiple team members are present, such as clinical rounds and diagnostic conferences, patients also take their artwork to continue therapeutic discourse with individual therapists, social workers in family therapy, and nursing staff with whom they feel connected. Individual therapy is a natural space for patients to explore their artwork in more depth. Though some non-art therapist clinicians appropriately feel inadequate in their ability to discuss a patient's artwork, the mentalizing stance offers them guidance, as approaching the image from a place of uncertainty, curiosity, and open-mindness allows for productive discussion.

These clinicians understand that the artwork is significant when patients take the initiative to bring it to individual therapy.

Following an art therapy session, Joanna asked to take a painting to individual therapy because it reflected themes discussed with her individual therapist. When she returned her artwork, she was asked what it was like to have her therapist see it. She responded that it felt good to show her therapist that she is reflecting on their discussions and processing their work in other areas of treatment. For Joanna, the artwork served an integrative function, providing a sense of cohesion among various components of treatment. Joanna's therapist also found the experience beneficial, and described having a productive session.

Another patient, Cathy, made remarkable strides toward mentalizing her family relationships throughout her time in treatment. She exerted valiant efforts to identify her role in conflicts and to reflect on the thoughts and feelings in herself and her parents. Specifically, she explored the tendency to idealize her father and devalue her mother. This split was illustrated in a collage she created in art therapy of her family driving in a car. Cathy and her father were sitting in the front, while her mother was in the back seat. During the art therapy group, Cathy was recalled exclaiming, "No wonder my mom was angry so much! She was cast out, literally in the back seat in our family." Cathy stated that she wanted to take this collage to her family therapist to continue exploring relationship dynamics.

Art, the empathy promoter

In this work, we are at risk for empathy fatigue. Therapists working with people who have personality disorders may be at high risk for burnout, possibly due to the impact of interpersonal deficits characteristic of these issues (Bateman and Fonagy 2016). We are vulnerable to compassion fatigue, and diminished interest and capacity for empathy (Adams, Boscarino and Figley 2006; Figley 1995). We bear some of the suffering of our patients, and the ever-present threat of burnout and vicarious trauma circles overhead, ready to swoop in and enshroud us.

The ease with which well-meaning clinicians are susceptible to acting with anger toward people with personality disorders (for behaving as people with personality disorders do) is daunting. It is still confounding when we are reactive and take personally the behavioral manifestations of patients' internal struggles. A particularly useful aspect of mentalizing is *examining countertransference* (Bateman and Fonagy 2012b), as our reactions are powerful indicators of what may be happening in the patient and what interventions are warranted. When we feel drained, we may avoid, become frustrated, grow irritable, and lose contact with empathy. Havsteen-Franklin (2016, p.148) writes, "it is perhaps not surprising that the therapist is able to empathize with material that is more readily available through the image than in verbal modes of expression." We concur that artwork is extremely useful in helping us attune to the affective states of patients, and regain contact with empathy. Artwork is a tool to refocus and recover our mentalizing when problems occur.

Ruth was regularly and appropriately described as a "difficult" patient. She had great difficulty in treatment. She was withdrawn and cold with her individual therapist, treating her with hostility. She was noncollaborative with her treatment team, evasive and curt with her nurse, devaluing of her addictions counselor, and often vocalized the uselessness of group work. Ruth seemed to unravel during family therapy sessions where she could be heard yelling profanities and having full-blown tantrums with her social worker and parents. The team experienced Ruth as mistrusting, hostile, suspicious, and dismissive of everything and everyone related to her treatment. Ruth acknowledged that her motivations for treatment were primarily external, as her parents had set a boundary that they would not pay for college if she did not complete treatment.

Due to the lack of traction in other areas of her treatment, and Ruth's interest in art, she was referred to the MBAT group during her second week on Compass. While she seemed to engage in art therapy and hold the art therapy space in more favorable regard, it became clear that any relationship developed during the six- to eight-week course of treatment would be tentative at best. Ruth arrived at the hospital following a suicide attempt but she was not able to explore the gravity of her suicidality in any arena of treatment. When she did mention the attempt, it was minimized. While she did not directly explore suicidality in art therapy, she was able to examine relationships with self and with others, revealing deep-rooted feelings of inadequacy and fears of abandonment, both of which underpinned the suicidality.

Figure 9.4 was created during Ruth's first art therapy session, where she made an image of her relationship with her treatment team. She drew several faces looking at her in a judging, criticizing way. The figure representing Ruth appeared smaller and was pictured pulling her hair and sticking up her middle finger. Ruth's peers were encouraged to consider what it would be like to be the figure in the center of the image, and they imagined feeling small, scared, anxious, stuck, and angry. Using the art metaphor to address the patient's defensiveness, Ruth's peers validated that they would also respond defensively in the same situation, given that the small figure was trapped and outnumbered by larger, more powerful faces. Ruth agreed that this was consistent with her experience of her treatment team, and reported feeling understood by the group.

Figure 9.4. Ruth's drawing of her relationship with her treatment team

As Ruth described the image, she provided a way for the group to see the world from her perspective and to begin to understand what her relationship with her treatment team felt like. Later it became clearer that this experience also applied to Ruth's other relationships. She described the surrounding figures in the drawing as critical, judging, unsupportive. She stated that the figure in the center needed to defend and protect itself because it was small, powerless, and distressed. Ruth identified feelings elicited from her image, including feeling anxious, alone, and terrified.

The art therapist brought this drawing to a team meeting and presented it to the treatment team. While it was difficult to cultivate empathy for Ruth, many members of the treatment team found it easy to have empathy for the small, enclosed figure in the drawing. Team members noted that the image provided an enriched understanding of Ruth. One member later offered that she could not help but think about how Ruth saw the team during interactions with her, because the image made a lasting impression. It seemed that Ruth's angry outbursts were now framed through the lens of her image: a small, powerless figure surrounded by perceived judgment and criticism and thus defending herself, rather than the icy, withdrawn, treatment-resistant, difficult patient she had previously been viewed as.

Given the severe and entrenched nature of Ruth's difficulties, the team maintained realistic goals for progress during Ruth's brief hospitalization. One of the changes evident during the art therapy process was Ruth's growing ability to recognize her absolute certainty and to challenge it. She demonstrated reluctance to exercise curiosity about herself or others, but seemed to grow in tolerance of others' curiosity about her. During a later art therapy group, Ruth self-corrected a statement she made, changing from: "it IS this way" to "it FEELS this way." That shift was a small victory. She became increasingly able to recognize and reframe rigid thinking. This was indeed a small but welcome opening to flexibility on Ruth's part.

Treatment team lapses in mentalizing

Even the best treatment teams are not impervious to splitting, breakdowns in communication, and lapses in mentalizing, especially where patients with personality disorders are concerned. This may be due, in part, to the patients' inability to appreciate different perceptions and emotions within self and others, which causes irreconcilable divides, or splits, between good and bad, black and white, all and nothing. As such, it takes a fair amount of emotional energy to treat those with personality disorders. Bales and Bateman (2012) identified several challenges, including the slow process of change, and the burden of anxiety about safety risks from variable crises with this population. Some people with personality disorders are particularly gifted at "knowing where to poke," as one clinician put it, "and when to poke, for how long, how deep and when and if to twist."

Treatment providers are aware of the conflicting feelings that these patients can evoke, and this often surfaces in team meetings. A social worker in direct contact with family members airing their grievances may be able to empathize with the family's anger toward the patient. An evening nurse, who assesses the patient's safety, has nurturing discussions, and dispenses medication, may feel protective of the patient. A group therapist who notices the patient's tendency to dismiss others, disrupt the group process, or incite conflicts among peers may feel wary of the patient, and so on. As good objects and bad objects emerge, some clinicians are deskilled and devalued by patients while others are idealized and praised. Splits are created, and through it all, mentalizing clinicians are called to maintain a mentalizing stance because problems among clinicians are likely to interfere with the patient's treatment.

Team members arrive at meetings with their individual perspectives. Just as patients are encouraged to hold different perspectives in mind, it is the function of the mentalizing team to do the same. Clinicians must try to understand the differing perspectives of their team members, functioning as individuals with a "united mind"

(Bateman and Fonagy 2016, p.171). As disagreements arise, it is crucial to recognize why they develop. Bales and Bateman (2012) give several possible reasons for splits in the team, including "the internal processes of the patient, poor team communication ending in fragmentation, team members' own personally unresolved transferences, and difficulties experienced by the staff" (2012, pp.222–223).

Interventions vary based on the cause of the splitting. When disagreements have little to do with the patient, more team discussion and intervention is needed. At times, consultants from other teams and other units are brought in to offer another perspective and to help the team organize its *united mind* about the patient. The presence of another clinician who is not directly involved can foster reflection, highlight the salient issues, and help develop integrated strategies to address dilemmas. When splits result from patient projections, a discussion with the patient is useful (Bales and Bateman 2012; Bateman and Fonagy 2016).

In the same way that art can help patients mentalize about themselves, it can also help the treatment team regain mentalizing and get back on track when problems occur. We are reminded of the countless patients who caused rifts and confusion within the treatment team. The value of artwork in integrating the team is illustrated in the case of Stacy.

Stacy was disruptive in the milieu. No staff member disagreed with that observation. She often stormed out of groups, slamming doors, yelling expletives at her peers and staff. The treatment team was divided. Some believed that this environment was helpful because she could learn new ways to interact with peers. They gave more allowances because of her complex trauma, which Stacy acted in accordance with, often regressing to childlike behavior in the face of interpersonal stress. Others believed her behavior was toxic to the milieu and alienating to other patients, who expressed great distress from Stacy's emotional storms. Her peers could not confront or challenge her, presumably due to fear of how she might react. Some of them joined in as she devalued select staff members, and the rest fell silent when she projected a love/hate dichotomy.

Stacy continued to struggle in treatment and with half of the staff divided as to whether or not she should remain in treatment, we were aptly nervous when we received the referral for her to join the MBAT group. Primarily, our hesitation stemmed from the location of the group, off of the unit in a different building on campus. Though (we) two art therapists would be present, being away from the unit removed the prospect of immediate nursing support. If Stacy became dysregulated, the therapists would have to call nursing staff to come and take her back. All of this was explained to Stacy prior to the group, and she agreed to abide by the group rules, to inform the therapists if she needed to leave, and to wait for nursing staff to escort her back to the unit. Her treatment team agreed for her to attend, and believed that she was safe enough to do so.

In her first art therapy group, it was a relief to find that Stacy engaged appropriately. She created an image that perfectly demonstrated her internal fragmentation and the team's mirroring of it. She drew herself as an injured figure wielding a bloody sword to defend against attack by fire-breathing dragons. It seemed that part of the team had empathy for the figure being attacked by dragons and wanted to protect her, while the other part of the team focused solely on the violent sword causing damage and hurting others. This split caused conflicts within the treatment team. Divisive questions arose: *How could we send away a wounded person in danger? How could we keep a dangerous dragon slayer who could wound others?* These questions illuminated Stacy's negotiation of her social environment. For the team, it was not easy to see the full picture from either side of the chasm. Stacy's visual representation of her internal conflict helped team members integrate both sides and make headway toward mitigating the split.

Don't take it from us, take it from our marginally less partial colleagues

We openly admit that our views on the benefit of artwork in treatment are not without bias. In fact, we have thoroughly staked our careers on this claim. Thus, our growing interest and curiosity in team members' perspectives of the artwork led to us asking them the question: *How does art impact you when it is viewed in team interactions?* The following statements summarize various colleagues' responses to the question:

Artwork registers for me in a different way. It solidifies my understanding of the patient. In several cases, when I see the artwork, my understanding is enriched. Art registers in an impactful way. It changes the way that I perceive the patient and helps me to see how the patient perceives the world. The images stay with me, in my mind, when I interact with them. (Team psychologist)

The art is helpful. It's nice to put a visual to the patient's experience. Otherwise it's just a verbal description. I'm a visual person, anyway. The art has more impact. It helps me appreciate the patient's perspective. When I think about the pictures, it helps my understanding. For me, it seems similar to music and how it impacts the limbic system. It's like you bypass the verbal and go straight to the seen and felt experience. (Team psychiatrist)

I feel excited when patients bring art in to individual therapy. I use projective stimuli all the time in testing, and understand that art can be a repository for emotions that are difficult to express. At first, I wasn't really sure about the artwork in sessions. I still feel less confident about exploring original artwork versus using projective tests. But I let the patients take the lead and approach with curiosity. I find that when art is in the session, it really deepens our exploration. We are exploring it together and the physical image is [a] catalyst for that exploration. (Individual therapist/psychologist)

I think the art greatly enhances the diagnostic process, to give visual expression and insight to what is being discussed verbally through the testing. Seeing patient artwork enhances my view of the patient and brings another layer of understanding to their lived and felt experiences. I think it is invaluable and would like to see it used earlier in treatment and incorporated more in individual therapy and family work. (Social worker)

It helps a lot. It helps me understand underlying issues, how they are thinking and their perspective. I understand better how the patient sees life. (Addictions counselor)

The life of the group process

So far, we have explored the life of the image in various arenas of treatment. We have described treatment team interactions with patient artwork, which tend to increase empathy and understanding by providing more readily available and observable material, organizing the team's thinking about the patient. In addition to the tangible art product, what happens in the art therapy group process is equally significant. The group processing of the artwork teaches mentalizing in a way that patients can carry with them when they leave the group. Demonstrations of curiosity, active interest, clarifying, and transparency provide applicable and practical mentalizing that patients can translate to other interpersonal interactions. Experiences of making themselves seen and known through the artwork can be corrective and empowering for patients. This was demonstrated by Jimmy, a patient who carried aspects of the group process with him outside of the art therapy room.

It was almost painful to watch Jimmy in the main lounge of the Compass unit. He was often observed alone, with a book or drawing in hand, eyes darting around the room, observing peers interacting with each other. He did not take action to engage with his peers and often retreated to his room when overwhelmed. Jimmy's social interactions were primarily reserved for frequent calls with his mother several times a day, initiated by both parties. Jimmy received encouragement from various members of his treatment team to have more interactions with his peers and to not isolate himself.

Jimmy declined these requests, describing himself as "damaged goods," "a failure," and stating that he "even failed at suicide." At the same time, he spoke about how lonely and invisible he felt. Jimmy had identified the "cool kids" in the milieu. He imagined that they would not consider him as a person worthy to seek out or connect with. He had no interest in asserting himself, if he was not wanted.

Jimmy was often tearful when asked to explore grave difficulties with social endeavors, at times sobbing while describing himself as a pathetic loser, and adding that it was even more pathetic that he cared about this at all. Jimmy recalled an experience of his mother stepping in to rescue him from his social anxiety. He described his mother going to his elementary school prior to his arrival, in order to instruct the other children to allow Jimmy to sit with them. These relationships, engineered by his mother, naturally dissipated as his peer group formed autonomous and organic connections. Well before emerging adult years, Jimmy was on the periphery of meaningful social connection, save for his mother who struggled to tolerate his suffering.

In the treatment milieu, this dynamic surfaced. Jimmy connected well with staff, but seemed to shrink among his peers. He perceived himself as boring and uninteresting, expressing intense distress with his peers. He was unable to sustain any conversations beyond brief exchanges. Jimmy worked individually with a social skills therapist who encouraged him to explore his interactions and to try to understand how his peers would describe his interactions with them. Jimmy was assigned tasks to practice small talk, and it was suggested that this might eventually lead to meaningful connections. Jimmy quickly became frustrated with this process, acknowledging his expectations for immediate deep friendships and the subsequent feeling of hopelessness when his attempts fell short of this.

Jimmy seemed to make some movement in art therapy. In contrast to his difficulties communicating with his peers in the milieu and in other treatment groups, he was very engaged in the MBAT group. Figure 9.5 depicts his *Relationship with self* painting, which he described as a black hole set against a colorful background. Jimmy stated that he felt like a black hole, a place where no light could live. He experienced himself as a drain on the time and energy of others. The watercolor background represented the brighter and more colorful others from whom he felt disconnected.

Figure 9.5. Jimmy's black hole drawing

Another image (Figure 9.6) depicted Jimmy's experience of social anxiety. He drew part of a figure with hands reaching up around his throat. Jimmy explained that he felt anxiety in his chest and throat, which are filled in with bright red watercolor in his painting. Though he wants to speak to his peers, the words become trapped and he freezes. Jimmy explained that the hands around the neck were his own, and explored how he gets in his own way. The elongated neck and aggressive gesture toward self were also suggestive of Jimmy's body image issues and self-loathing.

Toward the end of treatment, Jimmy created a black orb with light inside and small tendrils reaching outward, seeking connection (Figure 9.7). Jimmy explained that this image represented his desire for meaningful peer relationships.

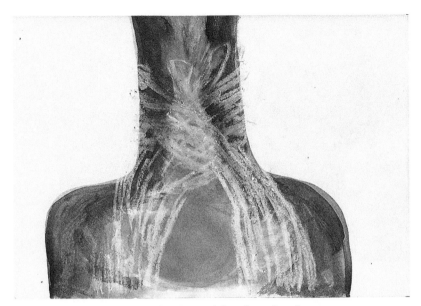

Figure 9.6. Jimmy's hands and neck

Figure 9.7. Jimmy's orb with light

In the art therapy group, Jimmy's peers expressed genuine interest in his art, which surprised him. Jimmy said that he did not expect to receive as much feedback as he did; he did not think his peers would find anything interesting about his artwork. The group seemed to offer Jimmy a chance to connect with his peers in the face of his intense social anxiety. It provided a space for him to be transparent about his struggles. He had a way of creating images that were emotionally evocative, and elicited concentrated curiosity from his peers, which combated Jimmy's beliefs of being boring and uninteresting. Jimmy's peers' questions and feedback might have allowed him to feel recognized in contrast to his sense of being invisible in his daily life. These experiences seemed to open doors for Jimmy to develop trust in his ability to interact with peers outside of the group. He became gradually able to initiate and sustain social interaction with his peers, and reported these moments of social competency to various members of his treatment team, who noticed an improvement. He became able to recognize moments of connection with his peers instead of dismissing and devaluing his attempts. The vulnerability present in the art therapy groups seemed to spill over into other social situations in the treatment milieu. Jimmy beamed as he reported that his peers laughed at jokes he made while in the unit's nutrition room, after which he sustained a conversation with a peer for a time. He stated that these experiences of social adequacy reminded him that he was capable of having meaningful relationships with people outside of his family.

When his efforts at connecting in the MBAT group were met with curiosity, interest, and empathy, Jimmy made attempts to reach out to his peers outside of the art therapy room. These positive experiences offered some scaffolding for Jimmy to take risks outside of the group. At the same time, art therapy did not occur in a vacuum, cut off from other aspects of treatment. Rather the collective experiences Jimmy had in all components of inpatient psychotherapeutic treatment contributed to his progress. The hospital setting provided Jimmy with a safe space and opportunities to repeat, explore, expand, and repair his patterns of relating to himself and others. It helped him to internalize mentalizing processes with improved ability to cope and regulate emotions, increasing trust in himself. Jimmy seemed empowered to problem solve and recognize more options available. He began to reconnect with hope.

Conclusion

This book illustrates the value of mentalizing-based art interventions in brief treatment for emerging adults with severe psychopathology and comorbidity, frequently including personality disturbance. Mentalizing offers a useful model for emerging adults, who are tasked with developmental goals that relate directly to interpersonal and intrapersonal functioning. These include identity exploration, clarifying values and worldviews, finding meaningful roles in society, and gaining autonomy and independence, while developing meaningful connections to stave off isolation during this tumultuous and critical stage of life. For emerging adults in the Compass Program, practicing and strengthening mentalizing capacity is an essential aim of treatment.

Arts-based interventions engage emerging adults in a captivating way. Art therapy promotes empathy, fosters curiosity, and reopens a pathway to epistemic trust. Art products not only aid in the patient's mentalizing, but also help treatment providers deepen their understanding of patient experiences. We have presented various group art directives used with emerging adult patients: mentalizing self and others, mentalizing attachment relationships, mentalizing the mind, appreciating differing perspectives, identifying core issues, and cultivating hope. We explored how mentalizing in the MBAT group is applied in other treatment areas. Our hope is that patients effectively make use of experiences in the art therapy group to enhance relationships extending beyond treatment.

A section in the *Handbook of Mentalizing in Mental Health Practice* is titled, "Don't Worry and Don't Know" (Bateman and Fonagy 2012c, p.68). In the beginning of this work, there was a sense of urgency to know, but we quickly discovered the value of *not knowing*, which is the pulse of mentalizing. We do not know and we are not worried. Instead, we have learned to pay attention to our own minds and the minds of our patients, to harness the power of art in fostering this curiosity. The primary aim of mentalizing-based art therapy is to maintain mentalizing and to help patients learn to reinstate it when it is lost. Equipped with training in creative interventions, art therapists can use this specialized knowledge to discover inventive ways to generate mentalizing in clinical practice. Art therapists working from a mentalizing framework are uniquely positioned to facilitate mentalizing in ways that other clinicians are not. We implore them to make use of this advantage.

References

Adams, R.E., Boscarino, J.A. and Figley, C.R. (2006) 'Compassion fatigue and psychological distress among social workers: A validation study.' *American Journal of Orthopsychiatry 76*, 1, 103–108.

Ainsworth, M.S. (1989) 'Attachments beyond infancy.' *American Psychology 44*, 4, 709–716.

Allen, J.G. (2003) 'Mentalizing.' *Bulletin of The Menninger Clinic 67*, 91–112.

Allen, J.G. (2013) *Restoring Mentalizing in Attachment Relationships: Treating Trauma with Plain Old Therapy*. Arlington, VA: American Psychiatric Publishing.

Allen, J.G. and Fonagy, P. (2006) *The Handbook of Mentalization-based Treatment*. Hoboken, NJ: John Wiley & Sons, Inc.

Allen, J.G., Bleiberg, E. and Haslam-Hopwood, T. (2003) 'Understanding mentalizing: Mentalizing as a compass for treatment.' The Menninger Clinic. Available at www.menningerclinic.com/education/clinical-resources/mentalizing

Allen, J.G., Fonagy, P. and Bateman, A.W. (2008) *Mentalizing in Clinical Practice*. Arlington, VA: American Psychiatric Publishing.

Allen, J.G., O'Malley, F., Freeman, C. and Bateman, A.W. (2012) 'Brief Treatment.' In A.W. Bateman and P. Fonagy (eds) *Handbook of Mentalizing in Mental Health Practice* (Chapter 7). Arlington, VA: American Psychiatric Publishing.

Antonovsky, A. (1979) *Health, Stress and Coping*. San Francisco, CA: Jossey-Bass.

Antonovsky, A. (1996) 'The salutogenic model as a theory to guide health promotion.' *Health Promotion International 11*, 1, 11–18.

APA (American Psychiatric Association) (2000) *Diagnostic and Statistical Manual of Mental Disorders* (4th edn). Washington, DC: Author.

APA (American Psychiatric Association) (2013) *Diagnostic and Statistical Manual of Mental Disorders* (5th edn). Washington, DC: Author.

Ardito, R. and Rabellino, D. (2011) 'Therapeutic alliance and outcome of psychotherapy: Historical excursus, measurements, and prospects for research.' *Frontiers in Psychology 2*, 270, 1–11.

Arnett, J.J. (2000a) 'Emerging adulthood: A theory of development from the late teens through the twenties.' *American Psychologist 55*, 5, 469–480.

Arnett, J.J. (2000b) 'High hopes in a grim world: Emerging adults' views of their futures and of "Generation X."' *Youth & Society 31*, 267–286.

Arnett, J.J. (2004) *Emerging Adulthood: The Winding Road from the Late Teens through the Twenties.* New York: Oxford University Press.

Arnett, J.J. (2006) 'Emerging Adulthood: Understanding the New Way of Coming of Age.' In J.J. Arnett and J.L. Tanner (eds) *Emerging Adults in America: Coming of Age in the 21st Century* (Chapter 1). Washington, DC: American Psychological Association.

Arnett, J.J. (2007) 'Emerging adulthood: What is it good for?' *Child Development Perspectives 1*, 2, 68–73.

Arnett, J.J., Zukauskiene, R. and Sugimura, K. (2014) 'The new life stage of emerging adulthood at ages 18–29 years: Implications for mental health.' *Lancet Psychiatry 1*, 569–576.

Arnett, J.J., Kloep, M., Hendry, L.B. and Tanner, J.L. (eds) (2011) *Debating Emerging Adulthood: Stage or Process?* New York: Oxford University Press.

Asen, E. and Fonagy, P. (2012) 'Mentalization-based Family Therapy.' In A.W. Bateman and P. Fonagy (eds) *Handbook of Mentalizing in Mental Health Practice* (Chapter 5). Arlington, VA: American Psychiatric Publishing.

Bachrach, L. (1984) 'The young adult chronic patient in an era of deinstitutionalization.' *American Journal of Public Health 74*, 4, 382–384.

Bales, D. and Bateman, A. (2012) 'Partial Hospitalization Settings.' In A.W. Bateman and P. Fonagy (eds) *Handbook of Mentalizing in Mental Health Practice* (Chapter 8). Arlington, VA: American Psychiatric Publishing.

Baron-Cohen, S. (1995) *Mindblindness: An Essay on Autism and Theory of Mind.* Cambridge, MA: The MIT Press.

Bartholomew, K. and Horowitz, L. (1991) 'Attachment styles among young adults: A test of a four-category model.' *Journal of Personality and Social Psychology 61*, 2, 226–244.

Bateman, A.W. and Fonagy, P. (2010) 'Mentalization-based treatment for borderline personality disorder.' *World Psychiatry 9*, 1, 11–15.

Bateman, A.W. and Fonagy, P. (eds) (2012a) *Handbook of Mentalizing in Mental Health Practice.* Arlington, VA: American Psychiatric Publishing.

Bateman A.W. and Fonagy, P. (2012b) 'Borderline Personality Disorder.' In A.W. Bateman and P. Fonagy (eds) *Handbook of Mentalizing in Mental Health Practice* (Chapter 11). Arlington, VA: American Psychiatric Publishing.

Bateman, A.W. and Fonagy, P. (2012c) 'Individual Techniques of the Basic Model.' In A.W. Bateman and P. Fonagy (eds) *Handbook of Mentalizing in Mental Health Practice* (pp.67–80). Arlington, VA: American Psychiatric Publishing.

Bateman, A.W. and Fonagy, P. (2016) *A Mentalization-based Treatment for Personality Disorders: A Practical Guide.* Oxford, UK: Oxford University Press.

Bateman, A.W. and Krawitz, R. (2013) *Borderline Personality Disorder: An Evidence-based Guide for Generalist Mental Health Professionals.* Oxford, UK: Oxford University Press.

Bateman, A.W., Campbell, C., Luyten, P. and Fonagy, P. (2018) 'A mentalization-based approach to common factors in the treatment of borderline personality disorder.' *Current Opinion in Psychology 21*, 44–49.

Bowlby, J. (1978) 'Attachment Theory and its Therapeutic Implications.' In S.C. Feinstein and P. Giovacchini (eds) *Adolescent Psychiatry: Developmental and Clinical Studies Volume VI* (pp.5–33). Chicago, IL: University of Chicago Press.

Bowlby, J. (1982) *Attachment and Loss Volume I: Attachment.* New York: Basic Books (original work published in 1969).

Brown, K.W., Ryan, R.M. and Creswell, J.D. (2007) 'Mindfulness: Theoretical foundations and evidence for its salutary effects.' *Psychological Inquiry 18*, 4, 211–237.

Caspi, A., Houts, R.M., Belsky, D.W., Goldman-Mellor, S.J., Harrington, H., Israel, S. *et al.* (2014) 'The p factor: One general psychopathology factor in the structure of psychiatric disorders?' *Clinical Psychological Science: A Journal of the Association for Psychological Science 2*, 2, 119–137.

Center for Behavioral Health Statistics and Quality (2015) *Results from the 2014 National Survey on Drug Use and Health: Detailed Tables*, Tables 1.22A and 1.22B. Rockville, MD: Substance Abuse and Mental Health Services Administration. Available at www.samhsa.gov/data/sites/default/files/NSDUH-DetTabs2014/NSDUH-DetTabs2014.pdf

Csibra, G. and Gergely, G. (2011) 'Natural pedagogy as evolutionary adaptation.' *Philosophical Transactions of the Royal Society B: Biological Sciences 366*, 1567, 1149–1157.

Dayton, T. (1994) *The Drama Within: Psychodrama and Experiential Therapy.* Deerfield Beach, FL: Health Communications, Inc.

Dayton, T. (2005) *The Living Stage: A Step-by-step Guide to Psychodrama, Sociometry and Experiential Group Therapy.* Deerfield Beach, FL: Health Communications, Inc.

Eriksson, M. and Lindstrom, B. (2005) 'Validity of Antonovsky's sense of coherence scale: A systematic review.' *Journal of Epidemiology & Community Health 59*, 6, 460–466.

Figley, C.R. (1995) 'Compassion Fatigue as Secondary Traumatic Stress Disorder: An Overview.' In C.R. Figley (ed.) *Compassion Fatigue: Coping with Secondary Traumatic Stress Disorder in Those Who Treat the Traumatized* (pp.1–20). New York and London, UK: Routledge.

First, M.B. and Spitzer, R.L. (eds) (1997) *Structured Clinical Interview for DSM-IV Axis I Disorders (Clinician Version) SCID-I Administration Booklet.* Washington, DC: American Psychiatric Press.

Fish, B.J. (2008) 'Formative evaluation research of art-based supervision in art therapy training.' *Art Therapy: Journal of the American Art Therapy Association 25*, 2, 70–77.

Fonagy, P., Bateman, A.W. and Luyten, P. (2012) 'Introduction and Overview.' In A. Bateman and P. Fonagy (eds) *Handbook of Mentalizing in Mental Health Practice* (Chapter 1). Arlington, VA: American Psychiatric Publishing.

Fonagy, P., Luyten, P. and Allison, E. (2015) 'Epistemic petrification and the restoration of epistemic trust: A new conceptualization of borderline personality disorder and its psychosocial treatment.' *Journal of Personality Disorders 29*, 5, 575–609.

Fonagy, P., Gergely, G., Jurist, E. and Target, M. (2002) *Affect Regulation, Mentalization, and the Development of Self.* New York: Other Press.

Fonagy, P., Luyten, P., Allison, E. and Campbell, C. (2017) 'What we have changed our minds about: Part 2. Borderline personality disorder, epistemic trust and the developmental significance of social communication.' *Borderline Personality Disorder and Emotion Dysregulation 4*, 9.

Franklin, M. (2010) 'Affect regulation, mirror neurons, and the third hand: Formulating mindful empathic art interventions.' *Art Therapy: Journal of the American Art Therapy Association 27*, 2, 160–167.

Franks, M. and Whittaker, R. (2007) 'The image, mentalization and group art psychotherapy.' *International Journal of Art Therapy 12*, 1, 3–16.

Fry, R. (2017) 'It's Becoming More Common for Young Adults to Live at Home—and for Longer Stretches.' Fact Tank, May 5. Washington, DC: Pew Research Center. Available at www.pewresearch.org/fact-tank/2017/05/05/its-becoming-more-common-for-young-adults-to-live-at-home-and-for-longer-stretches/

Gehr, J. (2017) 'Why the Affordable Care Act Is Critical for Young Adults: Low Income Young Adults Would Benefit from Medicaid Expansion.' April. Washington, DC: CLASP. Available at www.clasp.org/sites/default/files/publications/2017/08/Why-the-ACA-Is-Critical-for-Young-Adults.pdf

Greenwood, H. (2012) 'What aspects of an art therapy group aid recovery for people diagnosed with psychosis?' *ATOL: Art Therapy OnLine 3*, 1, 1–32. Available at http://ojs.gold.ac.uk/index.php/atol/ article/view/297

Groat, M. and Allen, J.G. (2013) 'Fostering secure attachments and mindfulness of mind: Syllabus for the adult division educational group.' [Handout]. Houston, TX: The Menninger Clinic.

Hass-Cohen, N. and Findlay, J.C. (2016) 'CREATE: Art Therapy Relational Neuroscience.' In J.A. Rubin (ed.) *Approaches to Art Therapy: Theory and Technique* (3rd edn) (pp.371–394). New York: Routledge.

Havsteen-Franklin, D. (2016) 'Mentalization-based Art Therapy.' In J. Rubin (ed.) *Approaches to Art Therapy: Theory and Technique* (3rd edn) (pp.144–164). New York: Routledge.

Hayes, S.C., Follette, V.M. and Linehan, M.M. (eds) (2004) *Mindfulness and Acceptance: Expanding the Cognitive-behavioral Tradition.* New York: Guilford Press.

Hendry, L.B. and Kloep, M. (2007) 'Conceptualizing emerging adulthood: Inspecting the emperor's new clothes?' *Child Development Perspectives 1*, 2, 74–79.

Holmes, J. (2006) 'Mentalizing from a Psychoanalytic Perspective: What's New?' In J.G. Allen and P. Fonagy (eds) *The Handbook of Mentalization-based Treatment* (Chapter 2). Hoboken, NJ: John Wiley & Sons, Inc.

Horvath, A.O. and Symonds, B.D. (1991) 'Relation between working alliance and outcome in psychotherapy: A meta-analysis.' *Journal of Counseling Psychology 38*, 139–149.

Josselson, R. (1988) 'The Embedded Self: I and Thou Revisited.' In D.K. Lapsley and F.C. Power (eds) *Self, Ego, Identity: Integrative Approaches* (pp.91–106). New York: Springer.

Junge, M. with P. Asawa (1994) *A History of Art Therapy in the United States.* Mundelein, IL: American Art Therapy Association.

Karterud, S. and Bateman, A.W. (2012) 'Group Therapy Techniques.' In A.W. Bateman and P. Fonagy (eds) *Handbook of Mentalizing in Mental Health Practice* (Chapter 4). Arlington, VA: American Psychiatric Publishing.

Karterud, S. and Pederson, G. (2004) 'Short-term day hospital treatment for personality disorder: Benefits of the therapeutic components.' *Therapeutic Communities 25*, 1, 43–54.

Kenny, M. and Sirin, S. (2006) 'Parental attachment, self-worth, and depressive symptoms among emerging adults.' *Journal of Counseling & Development 84*, 1, 61–71.

King, P.M. and Kitchener, K.S. (2015) 'Cognitive Development in the Emerging Adult: The Emergence of Complex Cognitive Skills.' In J.J. Arnett (ed.) *The Oxford Handbook of Emerging Adulthood* (pp.105–125). Oxford, UK and New York: Oxford University Press.

Konrath, S.H., Chopik, W.J., Hsing, C.K. and O'Brien, E. (2014) 'Changes in adult attachment styles in American college students over time: A meta-analysis.' *Personal and Social Psychology Review 18*, 4, 1–23.

Labouvie-Vief, G. (2006) 'Emerging Structures of Adult Thought.' In J.J. Arnett and J.L. Tanner (eds) *Emerging Adults in America: Coming of Age in the 21st Century* (Chapter 3). Washington, DC: American Psychological Association.

Lachman-Chapin, M. (2001) 'Self Psychology and Art Therapy.' In J.A. Rubin (ed.) *Approaches to Art Therapy: Theory and Technique* (2nd edn) (pp.66–78). New York and Abingdon, UK: Routledge.

Lambert, M. and Barley, D. (2001) 'Research summary on the therapeutic relationship and psychotherapy outcome.' *Psychotherapy Theory Research & Practice 38*, 4, 357–361.

Langeland, E. and Vinje, H.F. (2017) 'The Application of Salutogenesis in Mental Healthcare Settings.' In M.B. Mittelmark, S. Sagy, M. Eriksson, G. Bauer, J.M. Pelikan, B. Lindström and G.A. Espnes (eds) *The Handbook of Salutogenesis* (Chapter 28) [online]. Cham, Switzerland: Springer. Available at www.ncbi.nlm.nih.gov/books/NBK435815

Lapsley, D. and Edgerton, J.D. (2002) 'Separation-individuation, adult attachment style, and college adjustment.' *Journal of Counseling and Development 80*, 484.

Lapsley, D. and Woodbury, R. (2016) 'Social Cognitive Development in Emerging Adulthood.' In J.J. Arnett (ed.) *The Oxford Handbook of Emerging Adulthood* (pp.142–162). Oxford, UK and New York: Oxford University Press.

Leibman, M. (1986) *Art Therapy for Groups: A Handbook of Themes, Games and Exercises.* Cambridge and Brookline, MA: Brookline Books.

Linehan, M. (1993) *Skills Training Manual for Treating Borderline Personality Disorder.* New York: Guilford Press.

Malchiodi, C. (2007) *The Art Therapy Sourcebook.* New York: McGraw-Hill.

Masten, A.S., Obradovic, J. and Burt, K.B. (2006) 'Resilience in Emerging Adulthood: Developmental Perspectives on Continuity and Transformation.' In J.J. Arnett and J.L. Tanner (eds) *Emerging Adults in America: Coming of Age in the 21st Century* (Chapter 7). Washington, DC: American Psychological Association.

Michaelides, D. (2014) 'An understanding of negative reflective functioning, the image and the art psychotherapeutic group.' *International Journal of Art Therapy 17*, 2, 45–53.

Monaghan, M. (2013) 'The Affordable Care Act and implications for young adult health.' *Translational Behavioral Medicine 4*, 2, 170–174.

Moon, B.L. (1999) 'The tears make me paint: The role of responsive artmaking in adolescent art therapy.' *Art Therapy: Journal of the American Art Therapy Association 16*, 3, 78–82.

Moreno, J.L. and Moreno, Z.T. (1969) *Psychodrama: Volume Three.* Beacon, NY: Beacon House.

Napier, A. and Chesner, A. (2014) 'Psychodrama and Mentalization: Loosening the Illusion of a Fixed Reality.' In P. Holmes, M. Farrall and K. Kirk (eds) *Empowering Therapeutic Practice: Integrating Psychodrama into other Therapies* (pp.35–60). London, UK: Jessica Kingsley Publishers.

Neff, K. and Germer, C. (2018) *The Mindful Self-compassion Workbook.* New York: Guilford Press.

O'Malley, F. (2018) 'Intensive psychiatric treatment with emerging adults: Addressing the problem of establishing collaboration.' *Bulletin of The Menninger Clinic 82*, 3, 173–201.

Patalay, P., Fonagy, P., Deighton, J., Belsky, J., Vostanis, P. and Wolpert, M. (2015) 'A general psychopathology factor in early adolescence.' *The British Journal of Psychiatry 207*, 15–22.

Patient Protection and Affordable Care Act (2010) 42 U.S.C. § 18001.

Paul, M., Street, C., Wheeler, N. and Singh, S.P. (2015) 'Transition to adult services for young people with mental health needs: A systematic review.' *Clinical Child Psychology and Psychiatry 20*, 3, 436–457.

Pepper, B., Kirshner, M. and Ryglewicz, H. (1981) 'The young adult chronic patient: Overview of a population.' *Hospital & Community Psychiatry 32*, 7, 463–469.

Pettit, J.W., Roberts, R.E., Lewinsohn, P.M., Seeley, J.R. and Yaroslavsky, I. (2011) 'Developmental relations between perceived social support and depressive symptoms through emerging adulthood: Blood is thicker than water.' *Journal of Family Psychology 25*, 1, 127–136.

Poa, E. (2006) 'Trapped in transition: The complex young adult patient.' *Bulletin of The Menninger Clinic 70*, 1, 29–52.

Polek, E., Jones, P.B., Fearon, P., Brodbeck, J., Moutoussis, M., NSPN Consortium *et al.* (2018) 'Personality dimensions emerging during adolescence and young adulthood are underpinned by a single latent trait indexing impairment in social functioning.' *BMC Psychiatry 18*, 1, 23. Available at https://doi.org/10.1186/s12888-018-1595-0

Pratt, C.W., Gill, K.J., Barrett, N.M. and Roberts, M.M. (2014) *Psychiatric Rehabilitation* (3rd edn). San Diego, CA: Academic Press (original work published in 2002).

Rappaport, L. (ed.) (2013) *Mindfulness and the Arts Therapies: Theory and Practice.* London, UK: Jessica Kingsley Publishers.

Rubin, J. (2011) *The Art of Art Therapy: What Every Art Therapist Needs to Know.* New York: Routledge (original work published in 1984).

Salonera, B. and Benjamin, L. (2014) 'An ACA provision increased treatment for young adults with possible mental illnesses relative to comparison group.' *Health Affairs 33*, 8, 1425–1434.

Schaverien, J. (1999) *The Revealing Image: Analytical Art Psychotherapy in Theory and Practice.* London, UK: Jessica Kingsley Publishers.

Schulenberg, J.E. and Zarrett, N.R. (2006) 'Mental Health During Emerging Adulthood: Continuity and Discontinuity in Courses, Causes, and Functions.' In J.J. Arnett and J.L. Tanner (eds) *Emerging Adults in America: Coming of Age in the 21st Century* (Chapter 6). Washington, DC: American Psychological Association.

Schulenberg, J.E., Sameroff, A.J. and Cicchetti, D. (2004) 'The transition to adulthood as a critical juncture in the course of psychopathology and mental health.' *Development and Psychopathology 16*, 799–806.

Sheets, E., Duncan, L., Bjornsson, A., Craighead, L. and Craighead, W. (2014) 'Personality pathology factors predict recurrent major depressive disorder in emerging adults.' *Journal of Clinical Psychology 70*, 6, 536–545.

Shore, A. (2013) *The Practitioner's Guide to Child Art Therapy: Fostering Creativity and Relational Growth.* New York: Routledge.

Springham, N. and Camic, P.M. (2017) 'Observing mentalizing art therapy groups for people diagnosed with borderline personality disorder.' *International Journal of Art Therapy 22*, 3, 138–152.

Springham, N. and Huet, V. (2018) 'Art as relational encounter: An ostensive communication theory of art therapy.' *Art Therapy: Journal of the American Art Therapy Association 35*, 1, 4–10.

Springham, N., Findlay, D., Woods, A. and Harris, J. (2012) 'How can art therapy contribute to mentalization in borderline personality disorder?' *International Journal of Art Therapy 17*, 3, 1–15.

Tanner, J.L. (2006) 'Recentering During Emerging Adulthood: A Critical Turning Point in Life Span Human Development.' In J.J. Arnett and J.L. Tanner (eds) *Emerging Adults in America: Coming of Age in the 21st Century* (Chapter 2). Washington, DC: American Psychological Association.

Taylor-Buck, E. and Havsteen-Franklin, D. (2013) 'Connecting with the image: How art psychotherapy can help to re-establish a sense of epistemic trust.' *ATOL: Art Therapy OnLine 4*, 1, 1–24. Available at http://ojs.gold.ac.uk/index.php/atol

The Menninger Clinic (2014) 'Compass Program for Young Adults.' Available at www.menningerclinic.com/patient-care/inpatient-treatment/compass-program-for-young-adults

Tobias, G., Haslam-Hopwood, G., Allen, J.G., Stein, A. and Bleiberg, E. (2006) 'Enhancing Mentalizing through Psycho-education.' In J.G. Allen and P. Fonagy (eds) *The Handbook of Mentalization-based Treatment* (Chapter 13). Hoboken, NJ: John Wiley & Sons, Inc.

Verfaille, M. (2016) *Mentalizing in Arts Therapies.* London, UK: Karnac Books.

Vespa, J. (2017) *The Changing Economics and Demographics of Young Adulthood: 1975–2016.* Current Population Reports, April. Washington, DC: US Department of Commerce, United States Census Bureau. Available at www.census.gov/content/dam/Census/library/publications/2017/demo/p20-579.pdf

Wadeson, H. (2010) *Art Psychotherapy* (2nd edn). Hoboken, NJ: John Wiley & Sons, Inc. (original work published in 1980).

Wix, L. (2000) 'Looking for what's lost: The artistic roots of art therapy: Mary Huntoon.' *Art Therapy: Journal of the American Art Therapy Association 17*, 3, 168–176.

Wix, L. (2017) 'Studios as locations of possibility: Remembering a history.' *Art Therapy: Journal of the American Art Therapy Association 27*, 4, 178–183.

Recommended Reading

Acosta, I. (2001) 'Rediscovering the dynamic properties inherent in art.' *American Journal of Art Therapy 39*, 3, 93–97.

Arnheim, R. (1966) *Toward a Psychology of Art*. Berkeley and Los Angeles, CA: University of California Press.

Ball, B. (2002) 'Moments of change in the art therapy process.' *The Arts in Psychotherapy 29*, 2, 79–92.

Baron-Cohen, S., Tager-Flusberg, H. and Cohen, D.J. (eds) (1993) *Understanding Other Minds: Perspectives from Autism*. Oxford, UK and New York: Oxford University Press.

Bat Or, M. (2010) 'Clay sculpting of mother and child figures encourages mentalization.' *The Arts in Psychotherapy 37*, 4, 319–327.

Case, C. (1990) 'The triangular relationship (3): The image as a mediator.' *Inscape 13*, 3, 20–26.

Côté, J.E. (2000) *Arrested Adulthood: The Changing Nature of Maturity and Identity*. New York: New York University Press.

Eastwood, C. (2012) 'Art therapy with women with borderline personality disorder: A feminist perspective.' *Inscape 17*, 3, 98–114.

Fonagy, P. and Luyten, P. (2016) 'A Multilevel Perspective on the Development of Borderline Personality Disorder.' In D. Cicchetti (ed.) *Developmental Psychopathology. Vol. 3: Risk, Disorder, and Adaptation* (pp.726–792). New York: Wiley.

Fonagy, P. (1998) 'An attachment theory approach to treatment of the difficult patient.' *Bulletin of The Menninger Clinic 62*, 147–169.

Fonagy, P. and Bateman, A.W. (2008) 'The development of borderline personality disorder: A mentalizing model.' *Journal of Personality Disorders 22*, 1, 4–21.

Gross, J.J. (2011) *Handbook of Emotion Regulation*. New York: Guilford Press.

Gunderson, J.G. (1996) 'The borderline patient's intolerance of aloneness: Insecure attachments and therapist availability.' *American Journal of Psychiatry 153*, 6, 752–758.

Gunderson, J.G. and Lyons-Ruth, K. (2008) 'BPD's interpersonal hypersensitivity phenotype: A gene-environment-developmental model.' *Journal of Personality Disorders 22*, 1, 22–41.

Hass-Cohen, N. and Findlay. J.C. (2015) *Art Therapy and the Neuroscience of Relationships, Creativity, and Resiliency.* New York: W.W. Norton & Company.

Havsteen-Franklin, D. and Altamirano, J.C. (2015) 'Containing the uncontainable: Responsive art making in art therapy as a method to facilitate mentalization.' *International Journal of Art Therapy 20*, 2, 54–65.

Leclerc, J. (2006) 'The unconscious as paradox: Impact on the epistemological stance of the art psychotherapist.' *The Arts in Psychotherapy 33*, 2, 130–134.

Levick, M.F. (1984) 'Imagery as a style of thinking.' *Art Therapy 1*, 3, 119–124.

MacMillan, R. (2007) 'Constructing adulthood: Agency and subjectivity in adolescence and adulthood.' *Advances in Life Course Research 11*, 3–29.

McNeilly, G. (2006) *Group Analytic Art Therapy.* London, UK: Jessica Kingsley Publishers.

O'Brien, F. (2004) 'The making of mess in art therapy: Attachment, trauma and the brain.' *International Journal of Art Therapy 9*, 1, 2–13.

Rogers, C.R. (1961) *On Becoming a Person: A Therapist's View of Psychotherapy.* London, UK: Constable.

Roland, P.E. and Gulyas, B. (1994) 'Visual imagery and visual representation.' *Trends in Neurosciences 17*, 7, 281–287.

Schaverien, J. (1990) 'The triangular relationship (2): Desire alchemy and the picture.' *Inscape 1*, Winter, 14–19.

Schwartz, S.J., Beyers, W., Luyckx, K., Soenens, B., Zamboanga, B.L., Forthun, L.F. *et al.* (2011) 'Examining the light and dark sides of emerging adults' identity: A study of identity status differences in positive and negative psychosocial functioning.' *Journal of Youth and Adolescence 40*, 839–859.

Schwartz, S.J., Donnellan, M.B., Ravert, R.D., Luyckx, K. and Zamboanga, B.L. (2012) 'Identity Development, Personality, and Well-being in Adolescence and Emerging Adulthood: Theory, Research, and Recent Advances.' In R.M. Lerner, A. Easterbrooks, J. Mistry and I.B. Weiner (eds) *Handbook of Psychology: Vol. 6. Developmental Psychology* (Chapter 14). Hoboken, NJ: John Wiley & Sons, Inc.

Sharp, C., Wright, A.G., Fowler, J.C., Frueh, B.C., Allen, J.G., Oldham, J. and Clark, L.A. (2015) 'The structure of personality pathology: Both general ("g") and specific ("s") factors?' *Journal of Abnormal Psychology 124*, 387–398.

Silverman, D. (1991) 'Art Psychotherapy: An Approach to Borderline Adults.' In H. Langarten and D. Lubbers (eds) *Adult Art Psychotherapy: Issues and Implications.* New York: Brunner-Routledge.

Skaife, S. and Huet, V. (eds) (1998) *Art Psychotherapy Groups: Between Pictures and Words.* London, UK: Routledge.

Skodol, A.E., Clark, L.A., Bender, D.S., Krueger, R.F., Morey, L.C., Verheul, R. *et al.* (2011) 'Proposed changes in personality and personality disorder assessment and diagnosis for DSM-5 Part I: Description and rationale.' *Personality Disorders: Theory Research and Treatment 2*, 1, 4–22.

Springham, N. and Whitaker, R. (2015) 'How do art therapists structure their approach to borderline personality disorder?' *The Arts in Psychotherapy 43*, 31–39.

Syed, M. and Mitchell, L.L. (2013) 'Race, ethnicity, and emerging adulthood: Retrospect and prospects.' *Emerging Adulthood 1*, 2, 83–95.

Talwar, S. (2007) 'Accessing traumatic memory through art making: An art therapy trauma protocol (ATTP).' *The Arts in Psychotherapy 34*, 1, 22–35.

Yudofsky, S.C. (2005) *Fatal Flaws: Navigating Destructive Relationships with People with Disorders of Personality and Character.* Washington, DC: American Psychological Association.

Index

Art Therapy with Older Adults
Connected and Empowered
Erin Partridge

Paperback: £18.99/$26.95
ISBN: 978 1 78592 824 6
eISBN: 978 1 78450 940 8
152 pages

This book outlines a framework for art therapy with older adults rooted in a belief in the autonomy and self-efficacy of older adults, including those with dementia or other diseases of later life.

Advocating for a more collaborative approach to art-making, the author presents approaches and directives designed to facilitate community engagement, stimulate intellectual and emotional exploration, and promote a sense of individual and collective empowerment. Relevant to community, assisted living, skilled nursing and dementia-care environments, it includes detailed case studies and ideas for using art therapy to tackle stigma around stroke symptoms and dementia, encourage increased interactions between older adults in care homes, promote resilience, and much more.

Erin Partridge is an art therapist and researcher. She has worked with older adults for over 7 years and is part-time faculty in the art therapy department at Notre Dame de Namur in Belmont, CA.

The Handbook of Art Therapy and Digital Technology
Edited by Cathy Malchiodi, PhD
Foreword by Dr Val Huet

Paperback: £24.99/$34.95
ISBN: 978 1 78592 792 8
eISBN: 978 1 78450 774 9
416 pages

Interest in the use of digital technology in art therapy has grown significantly in recent years. This book provides an authoritative overview of the applications of digital art therapy with different client groups and considers the implications for practice.

Alongside Cathy Malchiodi, the contributors review the pros and cons of introducing digital technology into art therapy, address the potential ethical and professional issues that can arise, and give insight into the effect of digital technology on the brain. They cover a wide range of approaches, from therapeutic filmmaking to the use of tablet and smartphone technology in therapy. Detailed case studies bring the practicalities of using digital technology with children, adolescents, and adults to life and the use of social media in art therapy practice, networking and community-building are also discussed.

Cathy Malchiodi, PhD, ATR-BC, LPCC, LPAT, REAT, is an art therapist and author of several books, including *The Art Therapy Sourcebook and Handbook of Art Therapy* (2nd edn). She is the Founder and Director of the Trauma-Informed Practices and Expressive Arts Therapy Institute.

CPI Antony Rowe
Eastbourne, UK
April 04, 2025